ISBN 978-1-331-31313-7
PIBN 10172923

1 MONTH OF FREE READING

at

www.ForgottenBooks.com

By purchasing this book you are eligible for one month membership to ForgottenBooks.com, giving you unlimited access to our entire collection of over 700,000 titles via our web site and mobile apps.

To claim your free month visit:

www.forgottenbooks.com/free172923

DR. ROYAL A. MERRIAM.

THE

HISTORICAL COLLECTIONS

OF THE

TOPSFIELD HISTORICAL SOCIETY.

VOL. IV.

1898.

TOPSFIELD, MASS.:
Published by the Society.
1898.

REPORT OF THE SECRETARY.

In presenting to the society my fourth annual report, I have pleasure in being able to chronicle a continued increase in the membership, and a growing prestige among kindred societies scattered about the county, and in fact the state and nation. The year just closed has added thirty-seven members to our rolls—members who reside in thirteen different states.

We have lost two members by death, Mrs. Eunice Perley of East Boxford, and Mrs. Mary A. Colburn of Wellesley Hills, while four have resigned their affiliation.

Eight meetings of the society have been held during the past year and papers have been read by Sidney Perley, Esq., of Salem, Miss Marietta Clark, Benj. J. Balch, Mrs. George Warren Towne, the president and your secretary.

The society now has a total active membership of 271, resident in twenty different states. Every New England state pays its tribute. We have three members on the Pacific coast and one in the southern state of Alabama. An effort will be made during the coming year to largely increase our rolls and proportionately our income.

One event during the past twelve months comes to the fore with much prominence—the highly successful field meeting held on July 27th, the Essex Institute of Salem, uniting with us in extending a cordial invitation to the thirteen Historical societies in the county, to be represented at the gathering, and every one without exception sent its delegation, large or small. Methuen on the extreme northwest and Lynn on the southeast sent parties of enthusiastic antiquarians. A stranger within our gates, a Westerner visiting New England's shrines for the first time, left "Cold Roast

Beef Boston," or as we affectionately term it, Nahant, at the seasonable hour of five o'clock in the morning, and after spending the day in our midst told the reporter of a great metropolitan newspaper, that he had known the ideal New England country village only by what he had read and seen in picture, but at first glance he recognized in Topsfield a most delightful type. He had travelled the wide world over and never seen any spot more picturesquely rural than this same Topsfield of ours. At the public exercises in the afternoon the Town Hall was filled by an interested audience that heard eloquent speakers of national reputation. The Hon. Robert S. Rantoul, president of the Essex Institute; Prof. Edward S. Morse, administrative head of the Peabody Academy of Science; Gen. Francis H. Appleton of the Governor's staff; Mrs. Alice Freeman Palmer, ex-president of Wellesley College and an educator of national reputation; Rev. D. O. Mears of Albany, N. Y., the orator; Hon. Alden P. White of Salem; John W. Hutchinson, the famous singer of emancipation and other speakers of almost equal note, contributed to the unqualified success of an occasion that ever will remain a marked day in the history of our society. To unite the historical societies of the county at one common field meeting was something unknown in county annals. It remained for the Topsfield Historical Society to achieve this event and years to come will feel the good fellowship and influence of that July day.

But this society must not rest upon its oars and drift with the tide, for in the rapidly approaching year, 1900, must be celebrated with all pomp and honor possible, the 250th anniversary of our birth as a town, the 28th in order on the list of settlements incorporated in the Massachusetts Bay colony.

We should all take a wholesome pride in our honorable record as a town and make every effort to crown the anniversary of our natal day with a round of becoming festivities. It is perhaps none too soon to discuss at the annual town meeting the question of "ways and means," and even the election of a committee having power to outline the exercises of the day and submit estimates of cost at a future meeting. He who goes forewarned goes armed in all points.

A consideration of the matter in ample season may prevent mistakes of both omission and commission.

One other matter I would keep ever before your eyes—the eventual ownership by the society of a permanent home, a resting place in some ancient building, where our collection of historical objects can be housed and feel a natural growth, and where associations with the shadowy past may sharpen our appetites for things historical.

Such a movement must be made in the not distant future. It only needs the sinewy arm to guide the plow, for necessary funds will be forthcoming with the successful launching of the project.

Shall we not unite in bringing the question to a successful solution before the dawn of our anniversary year, the year when objects of historical interest will be most in repute?

Let a continuation of the good fellowship and earnest work of the past be hoped for in the future. Let our society be the spot where all creeds and stations can meet upon common ground, bound by a common tie of veneration,—a research into the storied past.

Respectfully submitted,

GEORGE FRANCIS DOW.

TREASURER'S REPORT.

Topsfield, Jan. 2, 1899.

The treasurer would submit the following report of receipts and expenditures for the year ending Jan. 2, 1899.

RECEIPTS.

Balance on hand Jan. 1, 1898,	$77.90
Historical Collections sold,	2.50
Binding volumes,	1.75
Annual dues,	97.50
	$179.65

PAYMENTS.

Printing,	$42.84
Engraving,	1.40
Binding,	11.44
Paper stock,	10.68
Postage, express, etc.	22.51
Field day expenses,	21.89
	$110.76
Balance on hand Jan. 2, 1899,	$68.89

Respectfully submitted,

GEORGE FRANCIS DOW.

NECROLOGY.

MARY A. (BLANCHARD) COLBURN was born in Shrewsbury, Vermont, June 28, 1824, and died at her younger son's home in Wellesley Hills, Mass., Dec. 26, 1897. She was the daughter of Stephen and Rebecca (Lake) Blanchard. On the twenty-fifth of November, 1846, she was married in Winchendon, Mass., to John Colburn, of Leominster. He died in Wellesley Hills, Dec. 15, 1886. Both are buried in the family lot at Leominster, Mass.

Four children were born to them; the eldest died in infancy; John Henry, who married Helen T. Bliss of New Bedford and lives in Boston; Mary Eleanor, who married Thomas Guthrie. He was born in Glasgow, Scotland, and died in Boston, March 12, 1897; Frank Martin, who married Ida E. Childs of Roxbury. She died Nov. 26, 1894.

Mrs. Colburn joined the Topsfield Historical Society in 1895. She was until within a few weeks of her death, an active, energetic woman, and maintained a lively interest in current events at large, as well as in the minute details of her daily life, the care of her son's motherless children, and the domestic duties which she personally supervised. She was the true type of a New England woman of the old school.

Her unselfish life and beautiful character will be a precious memory to a large circle of friends, and to the children and grandchildren who survive her.

EUNICE PERLEY, died at Boxford Sept 4, 1898, at the age of seventy-three. She was daughter of Thomas and Lydia (Guilford) Peabody, and was born in Topsfield Nov. 19, 1824. She married Humphrey Perley of Ipswich Sept. 16, 1844; and lived in Topsfield and Boxford. Her life was uneventful, and was wholly devoted to her family. Three sons, Elbridge Perley and Humphrey Perley, Jr., both of Boxford, and Sidney Perley of Salem, and one daughter, Mrs. Emma J. Chase of North Andover were born of this union.

HISTORY

OF

THE TOPSFIELD ACADEMY

BY

M. V. B. PERLEY.

THE LITERARY EXERCISES AT THE REUNION OF
THE TEACHERS AND STUDENTS OF THE
ACADEMY, HELD AUG. 12, 1897.

EDITED BY

GEORGE FRANCIS DOW.

THE TOPSFIELD ACADEMY.

HISTORY OF THE TOPSFIELD ACADEMY.

1828–1860.

INTRODUCTION.

To the Topsfield Historical Society was due the inception of the reunion of the teachers and students of the old Topsfield Academy, but to the enthusiastic cooperation of the students of "auld lang syne," was largely due, the instant success of the reunion, held on an August day, when Nature's brightest smiles strove to make the day one of dearest memory.

The morning trains brought many from a distance, and every winding road paid its tribute as the noon hour drew near. Lunch was served in the Town Hall, by resident students of the Academy, and an informal reception followed, with many happy renewals of old acquaintance; men and women who had not seen each other for fifty years or more, recalled the bygone days, and many were the effecting scenes and incidents. As the hour for the literary exercises drew near, a large number of students grouped themselves about the entrance to the Hall, and were photographed, in memory of the day. The Hall presented a beautiful picture, as flowers were abundantly used in decoration, the speakers platform being completely hidden by masses of ferns, sweet peas, and other flowers, and when the chairman, Jefferson K. Cole, of Peabody, called the assemblage to order, he faced an audience that taxed its seating capacity. Nearly three hundred of those present attended the old Academy at some time in its history. Rev. Alfred Noon, of Boston, offered prayer, and was followed by Mr. Cole, who delivered an address of welcome, in which he recalled many scenes and incidents of Academy

(1)

days.   Prof. John W. Perkins, of Salem, delivered the oration. His topic was the personal and local side of education.   This address was replete with timely thoughts, and was frequently applauded.   Prof. George Conant, of Pasadena, California, who was principal of the Academy in 1852, read an original poem. This was followed by the ode, written by Eugene Tappan, Esq., of Boston.   Mr. Nathan Dane Dodge, of Newburyport, conducted the singing.   Mr. M. V. B. Perley, of Ipswich, then delivered the historical address, an able record of the glories of the old Academy, that was greatly appreciated.   A reminiscent address, by Rev. George L. Gleason, of Haverhill, carried memory back to "the days that used to be."   Brief addresses followed from Hon. Israel W. Andrews, of Danvers; Prof. George Conant, who asked those present who were instructed by him, in 1852, to rise in their seats, and the surprising number, twenty-eight, responded.   Rev. Alfred Noon, John W. Porter, Esq., of Danvers, and Eugene Tappan, Esq., spoke briefly.   The exercises concluded by singing a hymn to the tune of "Auld Lang Syne," Rev. Francis A. Poole, pastor of the Congregational Church, of Topsfield, pronouncing the benediction.   Seated on the platform, with the speakers, was Deacon John J. Gould, of Ipswich, who attended the Academy in 1830.

The following committee, Justin Allen, M. D., Charles J. Peabody, Benjamin J. Balch, Joseph B. Poor, Henry W. Lake, Albert M. Dodge, Mrs. Sarah K. (Leach) Woodbury, Mrs. Ellen A. (Hood) Welch, Mrs. Catharine (Gould) Perkins, and George Francis Dow, members of the Topsfield Historical Society, or resident students of the Academy, arranged and carried to a successful conclusion the first, and probably the last, reunion of the teachers and scholars of the Topsfield Academy.

CHAPTER I.

THE TOWN OF TOPSFIELD AND THE INCORPORATORS OF THE ACADEMY.

Every mortal has his birth, his life, and his death, or as we are taught, his change of life, and after that the judgment; so, many human institutions, particularly those of mental and moral design, have their birth and life, and change in the sphere and manner of their activity, and after that a judgment.

Topsfield Academy is a case in point; she has pursued the common path, as if impelled by a common trolley. The day of her birth was one of joy throughout the grand old borough; her life was a gem, every facet of which reflected its own peculiar attractive color and brilliancy and beauty; her changed activity now lives hidden in a thousand measures of meal, and we, today, filial in our love and devotion, with breadth of view, cognizant of results, and just in our estimate (as she ever taught us), review her life and accord to her her proper meed of praise.

The birth of this institution was during an academical period. The spirit of education was rife; the time was opportune. From 1628 at Salem, almost to 1828 at Topsfield, when this Academy was instituted; from 1634 at Ipswich, of which town Topsfield was, eighteen years, a part; from 1650, the date of Topsfield's incorporation; from King Phillip of Mt. Hope to King George III of England, even to 1815, when closed the war that wrung from the mother country the last prerogatives of our nationality, the history of this people would be a well-written history of the wars. Indeed, it was the first opportunity, when the people, free in their nationality, big with the possibilities of free institutions, and persuaded of the value of moral culture and

(3)

practical learning as a corner-stone of an enduring republic, could hopefully, earnestly and practically, pursue and culti-vate the arts of peace.

At this time the spirit of education was rife—it brooded with propitious wing over the entire country. Time fails me to tell you of the Gideons, the Davids, and the Samuels, who, through an inspiring faith, wrought righteousness, escaped the edge of the sword, out of weakness were made strong, waxed valiant in fight, and turned to flight the armies of the aliens. Many of these men were college-bred; they were of high social culture, and they realized, as we did not, and as we cannot even now, the sentiment of the legend raised for years over the rostrum of the Academy: "*Knowledge is Power.*" They instituted public and private schools as soon as there were pupils to attend them. From that early day, during all the trying vicissitudes of ancestral life, the week-day when the school door was not open to the inquiring student has no date. Through all those years, school privileges abounded, as opportunities were possible, and means could be afforded. The public school was emi-nently practical, and the private school was no less practical in meeting a higher demand. There was no conflict, each rejoiced in the growth of the other, and each maintained her relative ratio of numbers. Gov. Dummer early scented the sweet aroma of this century plant, and endowed his academy in 1763; Phillips followed at Andover in 1780. A radical change in the common system was inaugurated about 1800, towns being divided into school districts, pru-dential committees chosen, and school work and government made comparatively definite and positive. From 1806 to 1820, Mr. Felt, the historian, counted no less than seventy-five advertisements of private schools.

At the time of the institution of this Academy, this cen-tury plant, so cherished and cultivated by our ancestors, and so hopeful in its fruition, was about to spread its broad pet-als and distill upon the balmy air the richness of its treasured sweetness. The common school, so recently established on its new vantage ground, was now to be supplemented by a permanent higher grade of moral and educational training within the means of the common people, and a permanent connecting-link between the common school and the college was to be established.

Nine academies in our immediate vicinity were instituted in thirteen years. "The Trustees of Merrimack Academy" at Groveland were incorporated Feb. 7, 1822; "The Visitors of the Theological Institution in Phillips Academy in Andover," Jan. 17, 1824; "The Proprietors of Haverhill Academy," Jan. 28, 1828; "The Proprietors of Ipswich Academy," Feb. 28, 1828; "The Proprietors of Topsfield Academy," June 12, 1828; "The Trustees of Abbot Female Academy," Andover, Feb. 26, 1829; "The Proprietors of Boxford Academy," March 4, 1831; "Lynn Academy in the Town of Lynn," March 13, 1832; "Beverly Academy," Feb. 7, 1835.

Topsfield was part and parcel of that ancestral avalanche of educational force. She had her Winthrop who left his name to a commanding elevation in the northern part of the town, and who, in 1642, sold for £250, 300 acres of land "situate in the hamlett, village or place called Toppesfeild* in the parish of Ipswich"; she had her Bradstreets, Perkins, and Peabodys; her Cleavelands, Merriams, and Cummings; her Goulds, Balches, and Howletts; her Hoods, Townes, and Averills; her Clarks, Lamsons, and Kimballs; a host of worthies. She appreciated the golden opportunity and rejoiced, as an Elisha, in the cast mantle of the fathers.

But besides these common inheritances, she had two others peculiarly her own. She was centrally located and "beautiful for situation."

The Newburyport Turnpike had contributed to the former of these for twenty-five years, telling daily the news and business of cities south and north The crack of the coachman's whip and the chuck of heavy-laden dray-wheels had been heard upon the north-west and west, for many years.

*This is the earliest known record of the name as applied to this territory. The phrase here quoted is found in a deed, dated March 20, 1642, and given by John Winthrop, Gent., of New England, then residing in London, England. to Edward Parks, citizen and merchant-taylor of London, England. The deed conveyed land whose south-east bound was six feet from the spring in the present northern boundary of Topsfield; whose north-west was near the old gate leading to the residence of the late Emerson Howe; whose north-east was probably just east of the Corp. John Foster estate.

Three stages passed daily between Boston, Salem and Newburyport, and one between Salem and Haverhill, and three
mails were each day opened.   This village was in daily touch
with every part of the county.   Here was the central relay
of horses.   Here were brought merchandise and passengers,
and political and literary conventions.   Here convened the
famous *Essex Junto*, Oct. 6, 1808, whose voice national in its
influence, waked the echoes of the *gilded dome* and vibrat-
ed along the corridors of the White House ; here followed the
great anti-*junto*, Feb. 20, 1809; here the Essex County Agricultural Society held its first exhibit, Oct. 5, 1820; here
was the great Lyceum convention, Dec. 30, 1829, backed by
such men as Edward Everett, Daniel Webster, and Horace
Mann ; here the Essex County Natural History Society organized, April 16, 1834; and here also the Essex County
Teachers' Association had its birth.   The central location
was an advantage of expanding value, and demanded stren-
uous exertions to be further utilized.

[Of the Lyceum convention, Hon. Daniel Appleton White
wrote : It was "a large concourse of gentlemen of influence.
I do not remember ever to have witnessed a more interesting
and enlightened assembly.   Very animated, earnest, and
protracted debates took place.   By a full but close vote,"
the following resolutions were adopted :—Resolved, that it
is desirable to establish a general lyceum for Essex County
—that previous to such formation, local lyceums should be
established in the several towns—that a committee be appointed by this meeting to prepare a circular letter and address it to suitable persons in each town in the county—to
call a general meeting to adopt a constitution—to draft a
form of constitution.   Mr. Vose was placed on the committee, and the meeting for adopting a constitution was called
at Ipswich Hotel, at 10 o'clock, on March 17, 1830.   The
object of the lyceum was "the improvement of its members
in useful knowledge and the advancement of popular education, by reading, conversation, discussions, dissertations, illustrating the sciences, or other exercises, which shall be
thought expedient; and as it is found convenient will be
procured a cabinet consisting of books, apparatus for illustrating the sciences, plants, minerals, and other natural or

artificial productions." The title used by the committee was Confederation, or Convention, of Lyceums. Topsfield had another meeting Jan. 18, 1830.—*Essex Hist. Coll., vol. 9, part 2, p. 50, and vol. 18, p. 293.*]

Her "beauty for situation" had been long recognized; her rural quiet and social amenities long attested; her village homes and farm villas indicated persistent diligence, a learned intelligence and stored wealth; the lake and river were an added charm to her landscape, and invited to aquatic sports; her hills afforded a great variety and extent of scenic beauty of land and ocean. Not, however, that she so far excelled her sisters; but that these natural gifts, each enhancing the value of the other, made her the first choice of towns for academic life.

Topsfield was a pioneer in establishing the new system of schools. "Miss Floyd's Academy" was located here as early as 1819*. Preceding this or succeeding it, or both and the while, was Mrs. A. P. Curtis and Lydia R. Ward's Academy. Mrs. Curtis' school is mentioned as late as 1827. The sessions of Miss Floyd's Academy were held at Dr. Nehemiah Cleaveland's house, and it may be that a knowledge of her success placed the Doctor among the foremost advocates of a public academy.

The original document, the initial formal action, in relation to this school, reads as follows:—

"Our country has already risen to a high rank in civilization and mental culture; and the present period is distinguished for the rapid improvement in almost every useful art

---

*We have been shown, by Mrs. N. Rawson Underhill, of Ipswich, a manuscript book whose title page reads thus:—"Miscellaneous Exercises on Composition by Lucy Martin of Salem, at Miss Curtis and Miss Floyd's school, Salem, June 12, 1816." The latest date in the book is July 18, 1819.

Abigail Floyd.

Informs her friends and the public, that she will open a SCHOOL on the first Monday in April, in the chamber over Mr. Stearns' store, Essex Street, formerly occupied by Mr. Blydon for that purpose, where she will teach Reading, Writing, Arithmetic, English Grammar, Rhetoric, Composition and Needle-Work ——Also an intermediate School from 11 to 1 o'clock.—*Salem Gazette, Mar. 17, 1809.*

and science. We the undersigned fully believing that the
town of Topsfield is very favorably located for an *Academy,*
and desirous to keep pace with the country, while we secure
to ourselves and posterity the means of acquiring useful
knowledge, *agree* to pay the sum or sums annexed to our
respective names, for the purpose of erecting a building or
buildings suitable for an academy in said town, the site to be
hereafter selected by the promoters of the aforesaid object
and whoever may have the munificence to endow the institution, it is our most cordial wish, and design, that it thall bear
His name forever, with the privilege of appointing, while
living, all the Trustees, of which body He himself shall be
the President.

Topsfield, May 8 day 1827.

Jeremiah Stone	$50	pd. $25
Thomas Emerson	100	
Nathl. Perley	25	
Frederick Perley	25	
Joel Lake	20	
Jerry White	10	
Corneleus Bradstreet	50	paid
Edward Hood	25	
Isaac Killam	50	
Moses Wright	20	
John Sawyer	20	
John Wright	20	
Benjamin C. Perkins	25	paid
John Lamson	40	" "

This paper seems to have been intended as a suggestion,
but their active purpose could not wait for respondents to
grow, and the following action matured in the next September :—

"We the subscribers do hereby covenant and agree together,
and do hereby severally promise to pay the sums set to our
respective names to be appropriated to the sole purpose of
procuring a proper site and erecting thereon, a suitable building for the exclusive purpose of keeping such high school
or schools therein, of either or of both sexes, as shall from
time to time be agreed upon by the proprietors or by those

to whom the management of the same shall be entrusted; and we do hereby severally promise to pay said sums at such times and in such proportions as shall be required by any committee duly authorized to receive the same, and it is hereby agreed that in all proceedings hereafter to be had in the premises, each subscriber shall be entitled to one ·vote for every twenty dollars by him or her subscribed, provided however, that no person shall give more than ten votes in his or her own right,——To the prompt and faithful performance of all that is above written we do hereby jointly and severally bind ourselves and our respective heirs.

Witness our hands this sixth day of September 1827.

William Munday	$100	Paid
Billy Emerson	100	"
John Rea Jr	100	"
N. Cleaveland	100	
Frederic J. Merriam	100	
Moses Wildes	100	
Jacob Towne Jun	100	
Samuel Gould	100	
R. Merriam	100	
Wm. N. Cleaveland	50	"
Solomon Wildes	100	
Gilbert Brownell	100	
Ephm Wildes	100	
Sam'l Hood	50	
Thos. Emerson	100	
Nathl. Perley	25	
Frederick Perley	25	
Joel Lake	20	
John Dwinell	100	
Isaac Killam	50	
Moses Wright	20	
John Sawyer	25	
Jeremiah Stone	25	"
Edward Hood	25	
John Lamson	40	
R. G. Dennis	25	

The building was begun in the fall of that year, but a severe cold coming on in October (when Jack Frost through out the country placed an embargo on unharvested potatoes and confiscated thousands of bushels), the lumber was piled till the next year. The structure was 45 by 36 feet on the ground, two stories high, was covered by a hip-roof, which was surmounted by a belfry in the center, whose bell one of the worthy instructors used to say was toned to the key of P. Each story contained a large school-room with ante-room and stairway. A writer, in the *Salem Gazette,* about that time records: "The building is perfectly and commodiously finished, in two departments, upper and lower, with blinds to the whole house. It is on an elevated, and most beautiful spot, a little retired from the public road."

The land was purchased of Dr. Nehemiah Cleaveland, 3 acres and 59 rods, for $637.50, and was conveyed by deed dated Oct. 23, 1828. An entrance upon the land was near the blacksmith-shop, in low ground, it is said, and unfitted for the purposes of a school. The present entrance on Main Street was purchased of John Rea, Jr., guardian of Harriet Josephine Emerson, minor daughter of Joseph Emerson (and late the wife of Charles H Holmes, Esq., long known as the tallest man in the county), 12.7 square rods, for $17, and was conveyed by deed dated June 10, 1829.

The following names appear in the act of incorporation: Nehemiah Cleaveland, who was a leading physician and in practice here many years; Samuel Hood, who was a carpenter by trade, a house-wright and master builder. He was master-carpenter on the Franklin Building, Salem, and on other noted structures,—and was chairman of the Academy building-committee, and the contractor and builder of it; Billy Emerson, who was the most extensive general trader Essex County ever had, and of whom it is said, he could journey to Canada (as he used to) and stop at his own hotel every night; Jacob Towne, Jr., who was town-clerk for twenty years; Isaac Killam, who was a captain in the militia and an independent farmer; Moses Wildes, who was a blacksmith and counted among the wealthy citizens; Samuel Gould, who was a grocer, and who exercised many town offices; Frederick J. Merriam, who was extensively engaged in both trading and farming, (is styled "drover," in the *Salem Gazette*, April 25, 1835); John Rea, Jr., who kept a hotel where Mr. John Bailey's residence now is, who was later of Portsmouth, N. H., and afterwards a farmer in New Brunswick; William N. Cleaveland, who was some-time a manufacturer at "The Mills," Byfield, and later a wealthy farmer in Boxford; Jeremiah Stone, M. D., who was a skillful physician, located in town about eight years, and afterward removed his practice to Provincetown, where he died; Moses Wright, who was a captain in the militia, and, it is believed a boot-manufacturer in Topsfield and in Georgetown where he later made his home; Edward Hood, who, in modern phrase, was a cattle-broker, and conducted a large business; Nathaniel Perley, who was a General in the militia, and kept a country store, till he sold to Benjamin Perley Adams, and removed to Danvers. The property is now owned and occupied by Joseph Bailey Poor, a general merchant. The act of incorporation further states that the above named persons together with such other per-sons as now are, or may hereafter be associated with them and their successors * * * * shall be a corporation by the name of the "Proprietors of Topsfield Academy;" that by that name the institution "may sue and be sued;" may have a common seal, and may purchase and hold any real and per-sonal estate not exceeding $30,000 in value, and may at any legal meeting make and establish rules, orders and by-laws for the well ordering and governing the affairs of said cor-poration provided the same are not repugnant to the laws of the Commonwealth, and may annex penalties for the breach of any such rules, orders or by-laws, and the said corporation is hereby vested with all the powers necessary for carrying into effect the purposes of this act; and further that the property of said corporation shall be divided into shares, and the proprietors of said shares, at any legal meeting may make assessments upon the shares for the use of said corporation and the same collect, in such way and manner as may be agreed upon, and all votes shall be deter-mined by a majority of the voters present, counting one vote to each share provided no one member, in his own right shall have more than ten votes, and the share of any proprietor who shall be delinquent in paying any assessment may be sold at auction for the payment thereof, by the person appointed to collect the same, giving due notice of the time and place, and after paying the assessment and all the necessary incidental charges, the overplus money, if any, arising from the sale, shall be paid to the delinquent proprietor, and the shares shall be deemed personal estate and the proprietors may establish the manner of transferring the same; also, that said corporation may appoint all necessary officers and with such authority as by their by-laws they may establish for the due management of its affairs and the regulation of the school; and that the said Jacob Towne Jr., may call the first meeting and appoint the time and place thereof: *provided nevertheless*, that nothing in this act shall be so construed as to prevent the Legislature from altering or repealing it at any time hereafter.

The term incorporators as used above embraces such persons as appeared by name in the act of incorporation, and they do not differ otherwise from the proprietors. The following is a complete list of the first owners of the institution, showing their respective interests or number of shares. It is noticed that the certificates were not cashed till a year or two after the school had its birth. All the certificates are dated Oct. 20, 1829, except the last three which are dated Sept. 7, 1830.

1.	William Munday,	No. 1 to 5.
2.	Billy Emerson,	No. 6 to 10.
3.	Samuel Rea, Portsmouth, N. H. (filled out and signed but not cut from stock book)	No. 11 to 15.
4.	Moses Wildes,	No. 16 to 20.
5.	Jacob Towne, Jr.,	No. 21 to 25.
6.	Frederick J. Merriam, as Rea's (No. 3) but indorsed: Transferred to Benj. Adams on March 29, 1830, for $15.00. Marked "cancelled,"	No. 26 to 30.
7.	Nehemiah Cleaveland,	No. 31 to 35.
8.	Samuel Gould,	No. 36 to 40.
9.	Royal Augustus Merriam,	No. 41 to 45.
10.	Solomon Wildes, Boston,	No. 46 to 50.

REV. MOSES PARSONS STICKNEY.

11.	Gilbert Brownell, Boston,	No. 51 to 55.
12.	Thomas Emerson,	No. 56 to 60.
13.	John Dwinell,	No. 61 to 65.
14.	Est. of Col. Ephraim Wildes,	No. 66 to 70.
15.	Joel Lake,	No. 71.
16.	Moses Wright,	No. 72.
17.	John Lamson,	No. 73 & 74.
18.	Wm. N. Cleaveland, transferred Sept. 4, 1830, to Rev. James F. McEwen,	No. 75, 76, ½ of 79.
19.	Cornelius B. Bradstreet,	No. 77, 78, ½ of 79.
20.	Samuel Hood, certificate cut out and gummed in again, and transferred to Rev. James F. McEwen, Sept. 4, 1830, for $5.00,	No. 80, 81, ½ of 84,
21.	Edward Hood,	No. 82, ¼ of 84.
22.	Rev. Rodney G. Dennis,	No. 83, ¼ of 84.
23.	Nathaniel Perley,	No. 85, ¼ of 89.
24.	Frederick Perley,	No. 86, ¼ of 89.
25.	John Sawyer,	No. 87, ¼ of 89.
26.	Benj. C. Perkins,	No. 88, ¼ of 89.
27.	Isaac Killam,	No. 90, 91, ½ of 92.
28.	Jeremiah Stone,	No. 93, 94, ½ of 92.
29.	Samuel Bradstreet,	No. 95 to 99.
30.	John Wright,	No. 100.

Benjamin Adams transferred shares No. 26 to 30 to Stillman Stone, under date April 3, 1830, for $25. They are marked "cancelled".

Wm. N. Cleaveland transferred shares No. 75, 76, ½ of 79, under date Sept. 4, 1830, to Rev. James F. McEwen.

The stock-book shows twelve certificates signed in blank by N. Cleaveland, President.

Jacob Towne, Jr., called the first meeting, of the proprietors and was treasurer till 1832, when Dr. Royal A. Merriam was chosen. Dr. Jeremiah Stone was the first secretary and Rev. James F. McEwen succeeded him. Nehemiah Cleaveland, Royal Augustus Merriam, Jeremiah Stone, Samuel Gould, Solomon Wildes, John Lamson, John Rea, William Munday and William N. Cleaveland were the first standing committee.

The institution was dedicated May 7, 1828, Rev. Rodney G. Dennis, pastor of the local church, delivering the address, which was printed. That was also the first day of the term. Mr. Dennis' address was well written, well delivered, and well received. The standing committee requested the manuscript for publication. It was published by subscription in a pamphlet of sixteen pages. Sylvester Cummings took twenty copies; N. Cleaveland, Billy Emerson, Francis Vose, Jeremiah Stone, Samuel Gould, ten each; Israel Rea, Jr., and Susan Cummings, six each; Joel Lake, William Munday, William Gunnison, Benjamin C. Perkins, Hannah P. Bradstreet, Samuel Hood, Jacob Towne, Jr., five each; W. N. Cleaveland, Benjamin Kimball, four each; David Lake, W. Conant, Thomas Balch, Cornelius B. Bradstreet, Nathaniel Perley, Moses Wright, Aaron Conant, John Wright, Lydia B. Emerson, Joseph Batchelder, Isaac Killam, W. R. Hubbard, Josiah Peabody, three each; eighteen others, two each; nineteen others, one each. The list of sixty-seven names probably shows, other things being equal, the enthusiasm with which the new institution was received.

The occasion was a red-letter day in the town's history. Mr. Dennis had spoken the right word; the school opened prosperously; the teachers were professionals; and the proprietors were in earnest and sanguine of success.

One of Mr. Dennis' opening sentences reads as follows: "Your attention is, therefore, solicited, while the attempt is made to offer some remarks, on the importance of connecting piety with knowledge. By *piety* will be understood a devout disposition of heart, accompanied by a course of life in correspondance with the divine commands, and by *knowledge*, the improvement of the mind."

Near the close he said: "This morning forms a new epoch in the annals of literature, and may we not say of piety, in this place. An Academy, in Topsfield, had, for many years past been a subject of conversation; many sanguine wishes had been expressed that there might be one, but never till now has one been opened. May we not hail its commencement, as a new occasion to the cause of learning, especially in this place? And may we not cherish the hope, too, that it will afford a fostering hand to that piety which as far ex-

cels mere human knowledge, as the unwithering glories of
Heaven excel the fading, perishing treasures of this life?
We congratulate its patrons on its establishment. The design does credit to your wisdom and public spirit, and the
accomplishment of it to your decision. The building which
you have erected is commodious and neatly finished. It
does honor to the superintendent and to the architect. The
spot on which it is located combines many excellences.
You have been no less judicious and successful in choosing
for instructors those in whom the public can put confidence,
both as to their literary qualifications and their uprightness
of moral character. May we not say, then, that this literary
seminary has been opened under auspicious circumstances?
Sustained by that wisdom, and public spirit and decision
which planned and created it; and in the care of so able instructors; and in the near vicinity of so many populous
towns; being easy, too, of access; and combining the advantages of salubrity of climate and beauty of surrounding
scenery, can we suppress the hope that it will flourish?
May the blessing of Almighty God rest upon it."

CHAPTER II.

The first instructors were Francis Vose, A. M., principal, and Miss Matilda Leavitt, preceptress. An advertisement of the school informs us, that she was "a lady highly qualified for the situation—the care of the ladies' department." Mrs. J. R. Towne, of Evanston, Ill., wrote, that Miss Ann Cofran was Miss Leavitt's successor, and left, she thought, when Mr. Vose resigned. She says, "I was a student at the opening of the Academy, and also during the Autumn of 1835, under Mr. Pike, who left soon after that term." The advertisement continues, that the principal had "been for several years past, engaged in the business of instruction", and had "fully established the character of an able, faithful and successful teacher."

Besides this recommendation, Prof. Vose had a reputation of his own. He had been, in some way, associated with his uncle Prof. John Vose, at Atkinson, N. H., the most distinguished teacher, says Dr. Geo. Cogswell, that Academy ever had. He married his cousin, one of Prof. John Vose's daughters, and thus became more vitally connected with the good name and work of his uncle. These things joined with his good ability and aptness to teach, creeping out quietly and widely into literary circles, made Prof. Francis Vose a very promising man, as governor and instructor of the new Academy.

The course of study, as in all academies, was arranged for mental discipline, moral culture, and practical life. The exercises of the commencement, Aug. 10, 1830, consisting of music, declamations, compositions and discussions, show that the Academy enjoyed a high degree of prosperity. There were twenty-one compositions, thirty-one declamations and an original hymn. These are some of the subjects treated, and the names of some of the writers and speakers: "Men may live fools, but fools they cannot die"; "Is public opinion a just criterion of moral character"; "The only amaranthine flower on earth is virtue"; "The world is infectious, few bring back at eve, immaculate, the manners of the morn". Miss Harriet Josephine Emerson told of "The Aborigines of America," and John G. Hood gave "Some reasons, why the custom of wearing mourning apparel should be discontinued". T. P. Munday declaimed of "Africa's future Glory"; George F. Choate, of "Mount Sinai"; J. G. Hood, of the "Cause of Missions"; and C. Cummings, of "The Grave". "The effect of Juvenile Libraries", was told by Moses K. Cross; "The importance of reading history", by A. F. Richards; "Love of Fame", by W. A. Peabody; "Lectures, a mode of instruction", by J. Peabody. There were discussions: "Does the King or peasant enjoy most happiness", by C. H. Roades and A. Gould; "Does the fear of law, or the loss of reputation, deter most from crime", by D. C. Gallup and E. Towne. There were these declamations: "Extirpation of the Indians", by M. K. Cross; "Talents", by E. Batchelder; "Influence of the higher classes of society", by P. Lovett; "Love of Country", by W. H. Lackey; "Slothfulness reproved", by C. Treadwell; an extract by G. F. Eveleth; "Solace of Hope", by M. B. Wildes; "Influence of Charity", by F. Cox; "Encouragements to Benevolence", by H. F. Putnam; "Nations of New England," by C Page; "Intrepidity of our Ancestors", by J. B. Eveleth; "Pilgrim Fathers", by A. Bradstreet; "Tomorrow", by J. Rea; "The Prize", by F. M. Lord; "The Cause of propagating the Gospel should stand on its own claims", by A. Gould; "Character of the Philanthropist," by A. T. Richards; "Right of suffrage", by S. W. Bradstreet; "The instability of earthly greatness", by R. West; "Protection of the defenceless," by C. H. Rhoades; "Resistance of the Colonies encouraged", by J. D. Black; "Tears of Science", by M. Wildes; "Obligation of Americans", by W. A. Peabody; "Intemperance", by J. Peabody; "Avarice in Government", by E. Towne; "Claims of the Colonization Society", by D. P. Gallup.

Besides these there were Latin and Greek declamations,

and an original hymn by Miss Harriet Josephine Emerson, which Rev. M. K. Cross says was very fine, far beyond her years. D. Peabody, also, gave "a short, pertinent and eloquent address."

At the commencement, of Aug. 9, 1831, there were fifty assignments: vocal music, nineteen compositions, an original poem by George Hood, two discussions, and twenty-six declamations—one Greek, one Latin, and two original.

Prof. Vose was a severe disciplinarian. He believed in the letter of the law. Dr. Cogswell, when eighty-two years of age [1890] related an instance in point. It was at Atkinson Academy, at the time the Doctor's youngest brother fitted for college, about 1820, or perhaps a little later. Four young men having completed their preparatory course for college desired of Master Vose the usual recommendation to Dartmouth College. But the evening before leaving, in violation of the school rules, they walked out with some of their female companions and school-mates, and the recommendations were withheld.

"What dire offense from friendly causes springs!
What mighty contests rise from trivial things!"

What lady indulging in reminiscence of academic life will not pronounce the punishment extremely severe, and what gentleman will not wonder what in contrast would be the condign punishment of the pretty features, grace of manners, and cultured intellect that Eve-like proffered the forbidden fruit! *Sic volvere parcas.*

It was, however, Prof. Vose's business to rear a careful man, an exact man, a just man, a liberty-loving and law-abiding citizen, as well as a thinking man in scholastic walks. Rev. Benjamin Howe, late of the Linebrook Church, who was a student a year under Prof. Vose, esteemed him highly and spoke of him as a dignified Christian gentleman, a pleasant and thorough instructor, a ripe scholar.

The Academy at once became a literary center, and Prof. Vose stood among the best educators in the county. It was at this academy, and during Mr. Vose's principalship, Dec. 4 and 5, 1830, that the *Essex County Teacher's Association* had its birth. Mr. Vose was the first recording secretary and continued in that office several years. There had been a preliminary meeting, presumably here in the June preceding. At this meeting in December a full board of officers was chosen and a constitution adopted. The annual and semi-annual meetings, by a provision of the constitution, were to be held here. The association was incorporated April 19, 1837, and the names appearing in the act of incorporation are N. Cleaveland of Byfield Academy (Dr. N. Cleaveland, of Topsfield, died Feb. 26, 1837), Benjamin Greenleaf, the mathematician, late principal of Bradford Academy, and George Titcomb, "Master Titcomb," as he was familiarly called, in Newburyport, where he first taught a private school and then the "Brown High School." The corporation could hold real and personal property to the value of $20,000. The association still lives, and as it has done in the past, so it is now doing, a good work. Mr. Jefferson Kimball Cole, now many years a teacher in Peabody, was several years its secretary.

At the same time the Academy was made a *Publishers' Repository of New Books.* In this it acquired a merited distinction. Here centered the learning of Eastern Essex County. About this pole revolved the interest of the reviewer, the critic, the litterateur. It was a thoughtful and apt use of the institution. Our nation then had no literature worthy the name, when compared with the world of letters. Nor is the fact startling! Colonial and provincial labors were works of necessity; there had been no time for anything else. But this, the period of which we write, permanently free from martial strife, was opportune for civic expansion. The national lyceums movement of 1829 indicated the popular sentiment in regard to literature. This repository was to supplement the labors of authors, by conning and pruning, by suggestion and commendation, thus enlarging the sphere, the influence and the value of their productions. The Academy was certainly in honor

Prof. Vose was taxed in Topsfield, 1829-30-31. A record places him in Topsfield as late as the first of December, 1831. He called a meeting of the Essex County Teachers' Association over the date: "Haverhill, Nov. 10, 1832." The programmes of the commencements 1830 and 1831 are beyond a doubt his. But Superintendent of Schools Albert L. Bartlett, of Haverhill, wrote, "Francis Vose was the Preceptor of

HON. ASA FOWLER.

and a chirography seldom excelled by modern schools. She died at the home of her son, Sept. 22, 1890, leaving two sons, George Thomas and John Francis, her only children. She was buried in the family lot in Pembroke, N. H."

The dutiful son continues: "My great grandfather was George Brackett, Esq., of Greenland, N. H. (born 1737, died 1825) who married Dec. 18, 1764, Ann March, daughter of Dr. Clement March, of Greenland, who, it is understood, was sometime consul at Madeira, and afterwards travelled in the Orient, and died at the residence of the American consul at Alexandria, Egypt; and whose nephew, Charles W. March, was a writer of repute and private secretary to Daniel Webster, when the latter was Secretary of State. George Brackett left a fund of $5,000 to the Congregational church in Greenland, N. H. $2,600 to the Hampton Academy, and $2,000, to aid in founding Greenland Academy, which bears his name. George's brother, 'Old Dr. Brackett' of Portsmouth was celebrated for his medical knowledge and skill. My great uncle Joshua Brackett was a Harvard graduate, and a doctor of repute."

Mr. Vose's labors are still cherished in Topsfield. His character left its impress upon citizen as well as scholar. He was helpful in civic life and in church as well as in school and among men of letters. He called his school together Sunday morning, for religious instruction; he instituted in the church a Sunday school. He was an able, energetic, all-round man; his school was a gem that attracted by its brilliancy and worth.

EDWIN DAVID SANBORN.

Mr. Sanborn was Mr. Vose's successor. His son Edwin W. Sanborn thinks his father "taught at Topsfield during the winter of 1831-2, and possibly nearly all that school year, since he taught nine months of his senior year at college". The New Hampshire Press Association Annual, 1884-8, says Prof. Sanborn taught, during his college course, 1828-32, in Brentwood, N. H., twice in Concord, and in the academies of Derry, N. H., and Topsfield, Mass., "continuing in the latter place a year after his graduation." Albeit the spring and fall terms of 1832 of this academy opened May 2, and September 5, with Mr. Sanborn as principal.

The term beginning in May agreed in time with his last term of his four years' course at Dartmouth College, and while he was passing his examination there. Moses Parsons Stickney* officiated in the academy—"a brief interval", wrote Mr. Stickney, "of four or five weeks at longest."

James F. McEwen, secretary of the proprietors, in announcing the Academy's opening, spoke of Mr. Sanborn as "a gentleman highly recommended for classical attainments and talents as a teacher"—a recommendation fully sustained by him in his long literary career.

In 1835, his *Alma Mater* elected him tutor for one year. He was elected to the professorship of the Latin and the Greek languages in the same year, and was professor of the Latin language and literature from 1837 to 1859. He resigned and accepted his election to the chair of classical literature and history in Washington University, which he occupied from 1859 to 1863. The latter year he was again elected by his *Alma Mater*—this time professor of Oratory and Belleslettres. He was librarian to the college from 1866 to 1874. He became professor of Anglo-Saxon and English language and literature, 1880. He received his master's degree in course; the University of Vermont added LL. D., 1859, and Dartmouth the same, 1879. Mr. Sanborn was born May 14, 1808, and died Dec. 29, 1885. Miss Kate Sanborn, author-

---

*Mr. Stickney, as a Congregational clergyman, settled in Eastport, Me. Afterwards he changed his views and was ordained in the Episcopal church, by Rt. Rev. Alexander V. Griswold, Feb. 25, 1841. He passed from deacon to priesthood, and as such became rector of St. Michael's church in Marblehead in 1842; then of St. Peter's in Cambridgeport in 1847; then of Burlington College, N. J.; then assistant minister in the church of the Advent, in Boston, in 1853, which he resigned in 1870. Thereafter he spent his winters in Boston and his summers in the rural quiet of his home in Royalton, Vt. He was born in Byfield, Mass., July 12, 1807, to Lt. Moses and Lois (Pike) Stickney, and died Aug. 19, 1894. His children were Anna Elizabeth Gray, born Aug. 12, 1843; William Brunswick Curry, born Jan. 16, 1845; Henry Stover, born March 25, 1849; Agnes Mary Palmer, born Oct. 5, 1851; and Cornelia Loring, born Aug. 14, 1861. Of these children only two are living, William a lawyer in Bethel and Cornelia a music teacher in Royalton, Vermont.

ess, New York, is his daughter, and he has two sons, lawyers in New York and Boston.

ASA FOWLER.

Asa Fowler, A. B., succeeded Mr. Sanborn. He opened the fall term of 1833, Wednesday, September 4th. He had just taken his diploma at Dartmouth. Dr. Nathan Lord, President of the college, thus recommended him: "Mr. Fowler stands in the foremost rank of scholars, is a man of very unexceptionable morality and of great industry and fidelity." He was principal here a single term.

Mr. Fowler was the ninth child in a family of eleven, and was born in Pembroke, N. H., Feb. 23, 1811. He married July 13, 1837, Mary Dole Cilley Knox of Epsom, who died Oct. 11, 1882. At the age of fourteen he was stricken with typhoid fever. Afterwards he attended Blanchard Academy, then in charge of Hon. John Vose, where he fitted for a teacher in the common schools. He worked alternately on the farm and in school. He studied Latin sixty weeks, and entered the sophomore class in Dartmouth College, where he graduated, in 1833, in the first third of his class. He was never absent from, nor unprepared at, any recitation during his 3 years' course. After teaching here, he studied law with James Sullivan, Pembroke, through the winter, and in March, 1834, entered the law-office of Hon. Charles H. Peaselee, Concord, as student. He was admitted to the bar in 1837; was elected clerk of the N. H. Senate in 1835, and had six successive elections; was U. S. commissioner of the district of N. H., from 1846; was member of the N. H. House of Representatives 1845-7-8, and chairman of the judiciary committee; was an independent Democratic nominee for governor in 1855; was associate justice of Supreme Court from Aug. 1, 1855 to Feb. 1, 1861, when he resigned; was delegate to the famous Peace Congress, at Washington, 1861; was law-partner of President Pierce from Sept., 1838, to April, 1845, and later of Wm. E. Chandler. He has drafted more bills for the legislature than any other man living or dead. In Oct., 1888, his children, William P., of Boston, and Clara M. Fowler presented to the city of Concord, N. H., a public library building as a memorial of their parent. The total cost of the gift was $25,000.

ALFRED WASHINGTON PIKE.

Alfred W. Pike succeeded to the principalship Dec. 3, 1834. The public announcements of this school had hitherto been made over the signature of the proprietors' secretary ; but now over the signature of Mr. Pike, as if he had hired the property of the proprietors, and purposed to make the school completely his own. He removed his family into town in November, 1834, from Boston, where he had been keeping a private school. He was taxed here in 1835.

Prof. Pike was a farmer's son, born in Rowley, March 21, 1791, to Joseph and Lois (Tenney) Pike. He graduated at Dartmouth in 1815, and adopted the teacher's profession. He taught classical schools and fitted young men for college, in Newburyport, Framingham, Woburn, Rowley, Boston, and brought to this school a ripe experience of more than twenty years. Under his tuition the school might have flourished long, but for a libel suit versus Beals and Green of the Boston Post. The Standing Committee of the proprietors— N. Cleaveland, Jacob Towne, Moses Wildes, R. A. Merriam, James F. McEwen, Nathaniel Perley, Jeremiah Stone—did all in their power to save the man and sustain the good name of the Academy, but merely nominal damages were not enough to disabuse the public mind, and Mr. Pike left shortly after the fall term of 1835. He died in Boston Sept. 6, 1860, at the age of sixty-nine years.—See further, Geo. T. Chapman's *Alumni of Dartmouth College.*

MISS ANNA SEARLE.

Miss Searle taught sometime between the principalships of Professors Pike and Greenleaf. She had taught a private school in Georgetown, D. C., for eighteen or twenty years, and brought to the Academy a ripe experience, eminent qualifications, and a noble Christian character and influence. She taught a full term, and no longer. She had "about fifteen pupils," says Mrs. Sarah A. Jenness, of Beverly, "of whom I was one. Mrs. Esther W. Hutchings, of Topsfield was another. Miss Searle boarded with Mrs. Susannah Cummings, sister of Moses Wildes, whose daughter Susan Cummings married Rev. Martin Moore, of Charlestown,

Mass." Mrs. Jenness continues: "Miss Searle was a lady of culture and intellectual superiority, and a conscientious Christian. Her intellectual and moral instruction was enduring. Her ability was not appreciated by the people."

Miss Searle taught, it is understood, in Newburyport early in her life. Mr. Isaac Wheelwright, a native of Newburyport, who studied for the ministry, and afterwards was an eminent teacher in South America and who died two years ago, at the advanced age of ninety-two years, attended her school there and thought a great deal of her as a teacher. Her oldest brother's first settlement in the gospel ministry, it is said, was in Virginia, and probably one led the other into that section. She left her school in Georgetown, to visit her father in his old age and sickness, intending, in due time, to return to the school; but her own health was failing, and, listening to the expressed wishes of her relatives and friends, she decided to make the home of her youth the abode of her declining years.

During this period, writes Mr. E. P. Searle, of Byfield, "Aunt Ann taught in the old Emerson Seminary, in Byfield, one or two years, a year or more in West Newbury, a town school near the Byfield Depot, and a winter term in her home district." He writes further: "She was a lady of stirling character, of strong religious faith, pleasant and good in all her ways." Mrs. Sarah H. Todd, of Rowley, her niece, writes: "She was a devoted Christian, and a lady of intelligence and refinement. She taught a Sunday school of colored children in Georgetown, D. C."

Her parental home was the Searle corner, near the site of the ancient Tenney grist-mill, and of the present Dummer saw-mill, in Rowley-Byfield. Her parents were Joseph, Jr., and Molly Searle. She had a sister Ruthy, born March, 23, 1784; and brothers: Thomas Colman, born Jan. 15, 1787; Joseph, 3d, born Dec. 2, 1789; Caleb, born May 21, 1792; and Moses C[olman], who was supplying the Byfield pulpit when he died. Thomas went to Madison, Ind., a six weeks journey at that time, and was settled three years over the first church gathered there, and died there leaving a wife and two children, who have now passed away. Mr. E. P. Searle never heard of his abode or labors in Virginia. Joseph preached in North Bridgton and Saccarappa, Me., in one of which places he died leaving one son now living in Niles, Mich. Caleb was a butcher whom the old people now remember as a marketman from Byfield to Salem twice a week. Anna was born Nov. 1, 1783. Where she was educated is not known. Her Christian methods in school suggest a training in the old Emerson Female Seminary in Byfield; but Rev. Joseph Emerson, buying the church edifice and remodeling it, opened his school in 1818, about the time Miss Searle began her labors at the national capital. She never married. Fourteen days before her death, she had a shock of palsy, dying June 11, 1841, in the house wherein she was born.

CHAPTER III.

BENJAMIN GREENLEAF AND HIS SUCCESSORS,
ASA FARWELL, WILLIAM F. KENT, EDMUND F. SLAFTER,
BURTON O. MARBLE, DANIEL O. QUINBY, JOSEPH
H. NOYES, AND KINSMAN ATKINSON.

The last record that we find of the meeting of the Essex County Teachers' Association at this place, is dated Dec. 1 and 2, 1835. The Association's meeting in 1837 was held Dec. 4 and 5, in the Court House at Ipswich. An advertisement dated May 5, 1837, reads: "Six small boys or girls may receive board, tuition and parental care in the family of the subscriber, James F. McEwen." By a pamphlet catalogue, 1839-40, Mr. Greenleaf taught the fall term and Mr. Farwell the spring and summer terms. It is inferred from these records that the Academy may have been discontinued two or three years from the time when Mr. Pike left.

However that may be, the proprietors chose an attractive name to open the "Second Summer term of 1839." Richard Phillips, as the proprietors' secretary, advertised it for July 24, "under the care of Benjamin Greenleaf, Esq.," and gave as references: Rev. James F. McEwen, Charles H. Holmes, Esq., Joseph C. Batchelder, M. D. No teacher was better known in the county or enjoyed a better reputation as a thorough, practical, and successful instructor. Mr. Greenleaf was a graduate of Dartmouth College, in 1813, and had been twenty-two years principal of the Bradford Academy, taking it with ten students and leaving it with one hundred fifty, and an enviable national reputation. While principal here, Mr. Greenleaf accomplished considerable upon that series of arithmetics which has made his name familiar throughout the land—especially the Common School Arithmetic, which has been imitated so much, but neither excelled nor even equalled.

(27)

Some three or four months before his death, which occurred Oct. 29, 1864, when he was 78 years old, the writer visited him. He was genial and busy as ever. A large ribbon-box from a fancy goods store contained the manuscript of his last book—a practical surveying—nearly completed. He lived in his loved employ, and was oblivious to all else. He had arranged a new multiplication table: "1 1-2 times 1 1-2 are 2 1-4; 1 1-2 times 2 1-2 are 3 3-4; 1 1-2 times 3 1-2 are 5 1-4, etc." This he repeated with as much ease as an ordinary school-boy would say, "Twice 2 are 4; twice 3 are 6; twice 4 are 8, etc." From every round of the mathematical ladder he would rehearse definition and rule with an accuracy and rapidity that would distance and surprise the most thorough collegiate. He spoke of Dr. Adams and his arithmetic, of Warren Colburn and his "Colburns"— of Adams with great respect and esteem, of Colburn with admiration. He gave his visitor two photographs—one of himself and one of Dr. Adams—and they are among the writer's choicest souvenirs.

The winter term began December 4th, and continued eighteen weeks. Joseph E. Bomer, who was many years a skillful physician at Ipswich, was a pupil, the term which began April 15th and closed November 5th.

Another pupil, Mr. E. R. Perkins of Salem, writes, that Mr. Greenleaf taught two terms, beginning in April and ending in October, 1839, and adds: "I attended his first term; the school numbered sixty scholars, of all grades and ages, from ten years to twenty-five; his nephew Moses P. Greenleaf, of Haverhill, assisted in the lower grades. Mr. Greenleaf was a rather nervous man; at times very active; and his clear, ringing voice would make the old academy ring when a boy forgot to behave. He had a habit of smoothing down a boy's face heavily with his palm, if the boy was caught whispering. He always opened school with prayer and used the same one continually, full half the time scanning every desk with his keen eyes. He used his own arithmetic, and boys asking assistance he delighted to put off with a cunning smile on his face, and the kindly injunction: 'Puzzle it out.' "

Mrs. Ellen F. (Kimball) Morgan writes as follows: "By

BENJAMIN GREENLEAF.

a mere chance, I found among some old papers an original catalogue of the Academy, issued in 1840, by that celebrated mathematician, Benjamin Greenleaf, A. M., who was principal in the fall term of that year, and Asa Farwell, A. B., principal of the winter and summer terms. The number of students was—gentlemen 58, and ladies 46. One of the gentlemen was Geronimo Sigaroly, from St. Jago, Cuba. Can any of those who attended school at the time give any information in regard to the Spanish student, who drifted into this quiet village from that fair island of the tropics? In comparing the old catalogue with those of 1857 and '58, by Profs. Healy and Allis, I find nearly the same inducements, as healthfulness of locality, over-sight of students, and other minor items, but the course of study suffers, in comparison, not so much in the classical department as in the English. We never found a more puzzling, yet practical arithmetic than Mr. Greenleaf's. His algebra was used extensively in the schools at a later date. The curriculum was narrow in other respects, when compared with the branches taught from 1855 to 1859."

After leaving this institution, he conducted the Bradford Teacher's Seminary, which was doubtless suggested by the discussions of the Essex County Teachers' Association, of which he was one of the founders.

The wisdom of the proprietors of the school to employ Mr. Greenleaf became apparent. He established its old-time reputation, the old grounds re-echoed with the voices of many students, and the halls were devoted to patient study. It became an attraction alike to scholars and teachers of character and ability.

ASA FARWELL.

Mr. Greenleaf was succeeded by Asa Farwell, A .B. J. C. Batchelder, Secretary, March 7, 1840, announced the next term of the school to begin April 15, 1840, under the care of "the present Principal, Mr. Asa Farwell, A. B." He began the preceding winter term.

Mr. E. R. Perkins, of Salem, one of his pupils, wrote: "He was admired by his scholars, as a teacher and a gentleman." Mr. Thomas K. Leach, of Topsfield, said: "He was a fine man and an excellent teacher." Rev. Calvin E. Park, of West Boxford, wrote: "He was held in high estimation both as to talents and character."

"Asa Farwell," wrote his widow from Easthamptom, "taught at Topsfield one year—1840-1. He was born to Gurdon and Anna (Farnsworth) Farwell, in Dorset, Vt., March 8, 1812. He fitted for college under his pastor, Rev. William Jackson, D. D., at Dorset, and at Burr Seminary, Manchester, Vt. He graduated at Middlebury College, 1838, and at Andover Theological Seminary in 1842. He was approbated to preach by the Andover Association, in the spring of that year. From May, 1842, to Nov., 1853, he was principal of Abbot Academy, Andover. He traveled in Europe during a portion of 1849-50. He was ordained April 12, 1853, and installed pastor of the Congregational church, in West Haverhill, and dismissed in 1856. He preached in Bentonport, on the Des Moines, Iowa, from 1866 to 1871, when he went to Ashland, 24 miles from Lincoln, Nebraska. In 1877, he became professor in Doane College, Crete, Nebraska. In 1881, he returned, in ill health, to Dorset, and in 1882 retired to Ludlow, where his son, Charles Gurdon Farwell, was principal of Black River Academy. He died suddenly, of paralysis of the heart, May 14, 1888, in his 77th year.

"There have doubtless been many men of more showy, and among a large class of people of more popular, talent than he; but for sound scholarship and solid good sense, for clear and scriptural views of evangelical faith, for sincere and devoted piety, for honest and faithful service as a minister, very few men have excelled him."

His first wife was Hannah Sexton, of Windsor, Ct., who was married Dec. 10, 1845, and died Sept. 4, 1848. His second wife was her sister Mary Ann Sexton, who was married Aug. 10, 1849, and with four sons of his six children survives him.

WILLIAM FAYETTE KENT.

William Fayette Kent followed Prof. Farwell. He was born in Dorset, Vt., in July, 1820, and graduated at Middlebury College, in 1839. He was principal of Bennington Academy, 1839-40, and probably taught here next; he was taxed here, as was Mr. Farwell, in 1841. He taught nearly two terms. He was a very pleasant man and teacher, but was reading law at the time and paid more attention to his illustrious namesake and Blackstone than to his school. The inevitable result followed. He left the school before the timely ending of the term. It is said he read law in Salem. For some years he was a mercantile agent in the West and South. In 1851, he resided in Zanesville, O. He died in 1856—probably in St. Louis, Mo. He was an energetic man, a fine scholar, and a brilliant speaker. He delivered an oration at a Fourth of July celebration in Topsfield, and Hon. Asahel Huntington, Otis P. Lord, Esq., (afterwards Judge Lord) and Secretary Crowninshield of the U. S. Navy, were some of the dignitaries who graced the occasion.

Mr. Humphrey Balch, of Topsfield, very highly complimented his effort on that occassion, in giving us some account of the celebration, and Mr. E. R. Perkins wrote: "He was a fine orator. His oration was an eloquent production and was widely commented upon and praised."

EDMUND FARWELL SLAFTER.

Mr. Slafter was principal of the Academy one year, he says, beginning in the autumn of 1841, and ending with the summer term of 1842. He was born May 30, 1816, and graduated at Dartmouth in 1840. "As a teacher, he was liked very well," wrote one of his pupils. He has gained celebrity in the pulpit, and is widely known as an archæologist, whose authority is in high repute. He was ordained by the Rt. Rev. Manton Eastburne, D. D., July 12, 1844; was Rector of St. Peter's church, Cambridge, two years; of St. John's, Jamaica Plain, 1846-53; was superintendent in the American Bible Society of the Protestant Episcopal church, twenty years; is a member of the Mass. Historical Society; Royal Historical Society of England; president of the Prince Society, and has been a member of its council from its organization in 1858; is registrar of the Diocese of Massachusetts, and has issued six annual reports; and is corresponding secretary of the Mass. Bible Society and chairman of its prudential committee. He has numerous publications: Death of

Gen. Zachary Taylor; Planting and Growth of Episcopal Church; Slafter Genealogy; Assassination Plot of 1776; Charter of Norwich, Vt.; Vermont Coinage; Anniversary of the Historic-Genealogical Society; Copper Coinage, 1632; Pre-historic Copper Implements; Voyages of the Norsemen; Voyages of Champlain; Incorrect Latitudes, 1535-1740; Royal Arms, Emblems, Memorials; Norman Discovery of America; making 17 volumes in all. He now resides in Boston, at the age of 83 years.

Joseph Edward Bomer was an assistant to Mr. Slafter. Mrs. S. A. Jenness, of Beverly, writes, that young Bomer was a member of the Academy in 1839, when Mr. Greenleaf taught. She was a student at the time. She speaks in praise of young Bomer's perseverance. He walked to the Academy from Wenham daily. He began to teach in the winter of 1839 (in Hamilton, she thinks) and was recommended by Mr. Greenleaf. His first school was a great success.

Assistant Bomer was born in Beverly March 14, 1819, the fifth son in a family of nine children. His father, John S. Bomer, was a farmer, and of French descent. Joseph inherited a delicate constitution; he was fond of books; and was devoted to intellectual pursuits. He was a student under the tuition of Prof. Slafter, who became very much attached to him, and later on engaged him as assistant. Mr. Slafter, under date of Nov. 10, 1842, thus commended him:—

"This may certify that Mr. Joseph E. Bomer has been a member of this institution seven months, has made good attainments in study, is a young man of great perseverance and of good promise. He possesses an unimpeachable moral character, is dignified and courteous in his manners and worthy the highest esteem. He has read under my tuition several of Cicero's orations, and a part of the Ænead of Virgil; likewise the introductory exercises, the fables, and 120 paragraphs of Jacob's Greek Reader; also Day's Algebra as far as infinitesimals, working all the problems. He has been a successful teacher, and I can most cheerfully recommend him as being well qualified to instruct in any town school agreeably to the laws of any of the New England States."

REV. EDMUND F. SLAFTER.

He afterwards studied in Phillips Exeter and Phillips Andover Academies and Harvard Medical School, graduating from the latter in 1848. In 1849, he settled in Ipswich. He located near the residence of Dr. Thomas Manning, the oldest and most skillful physician in the town. Dr. Bomer married Caroline Elizabeth Hayes, daughter of Daniel Hayes, of Gloucester (who now resides in Ipswich), Oct. 23, 1850, and soon after, Dr. Manning, feeling the burden of his age and profession, invited the young doctor to reside with him and assume his practice. The offer was accepted and they lived in reciprocal confidence to the end. Dr. Bomer was physician to the House of Correction till his death, examining surgeon during the Rebellion, and member of the school board many years. He was one of the founders of the Episcopal Church and society and an earnest supporter of them. "A beautiful memorial window was placed in the chancel of the church, by Rev. Dr. John Cotton Smith, as a sacred memorial of his love and devotion to the church." He was a genial, sympathetic, Christian gentleman, and was eminently a public spirited citizen, and foremost in all works of public utility. He died in Ipswich, Sept. 11, 1864, aged forty-five years.

BURTON ONESIPHORUS MARBLE.

Mr. Marble was taxed in Topsfield in 1844, and by that fact we understand he taught the Academy during the spring term of that year. Mr. E. R. Perkins, of Salem, says, Mr. Marble began with the fall term of 1843 and taught through the winter and spring, but is not sure that he taught the following summer. He was born in Bradford, Feb. 27, 1812, and graduated at Dartmouth College, 1838, dying at Dover, N. H., July 12, 1845, says Chapman's Dartmouth Alumni.

Mr. Perkins continues: "He was very sober, stiff, sedate; and was a very thorough teacher—he was thorough in everything he taught; the lessons assigned were exactly defined and to be thoroughly learned—it had to be done. He allowed no whispering. It was the stillest school I was ever in. Each scholar had to keep a record of his daily work— of his errors and whispers. When a question was missed, he would say, 'You will please record an error.' The records were examined once a week.   He was a teacher to be re-spected."

DANIEL OSGOOD QUINBY.

Prof. Quinby was taxed in Topsfield in 1845, and it is in-ferred from that fact, that he taught the spring or summer term of that year.   His service ended with the summer term in June, 1846.   A correspondent writes: "Some thought he was too familiar with his scholars; he liked to play foot-ball with them, and was fond of athletic sports.   At the close of the last term, he announced to the school, when the next term would begin.   The old bell rang the call but he never responded."

Mr. Quinby was born in Amesbury, Dec. 21, 1821.   His parents were Capt. Robert and Abigail, who owned large farming interests.   His mother was a daughter of Orlando Sargent.   She was a sister of Mrs. Sally Weed, who was 100 years old, Jan. 28, 1898, and is now living in Merrimac. Her younger brother Francis, was of the firm of Francis Sargent & Co., carriage manufacturers, Boston.

Daniel Quinby attended Dummer Academy five years, un-der the tuition of Master Nehemiah Cleaveland.   Joseph H. Noyes, the next principal of the Topsfield Academy, was a classmate.   Mr. Quinby graduated at Bowdoin College in 1839.   In his class were the the late Judge Choate of Salem, Hon. William D. Northend, also of Salem, and W. W. Cald well, of Newburyport

Directly after graduation and while a law-student, he taught school two years in Maine.   Then returning home to Amesbury, he sought and obtained the principalship of the Topsfield Academy.   The office, however, not proving suf-ficiently remunerative, he resigned at the end of the school year, June, 1846.

After leaving the Academy, he was engaged, as teacher, in Watertown, Mass.; High school, Dover, N. H.; Norwich Academy, Ct.; Union-Hall Academy, Jamaica, L. I.; and was sometime professor of chemistry in New York City. During the last dozen years of his life, he was engaged in a proprietary medicine business.

Mr. Quinby married, Nov. 25, 1859, Miss Clara Belle

Moulton, sister of H. W. Moulton, Esq., of Newburyport, and had five children, four of whom died in infancy. His eldest child was a lady of great promise, residing, at the age of twenty-one (1890), in Paterson, N. J. Mrs. Quinby died in Boston, Nov. 30, 1882 at the age of fifty-six years. Mr. Quinby died of paralysis of the brain, in Haverhill, Mass., at the home of his brother, Thomas W. Quinby, Dec. 23, 1894, at the age of seventy-three years and a day. The remains of all his dead repose in the Belleville Cemetery, Newburyport, near the old Amesbury cemetery where lies the ashes of their ancestors for the last two hundred and forty-six years.

JOSEPH HALE NOYES.

Mr. Noyes taught three terms in the year 1846, beginning in March or April. He was born in Byfield Parish, Newbury, May 12, 1825, to Dea. Daniel and Mary Hale (Parish) Noyes, who was a daughter of Rev. Elijah Parish, distinguished in clerical circles throughout the state, as author and preacher. The family comprised eight sons and two daughters.

Joseph was educated at Dummer Academy, and was probably admitted there at an earlier age than any other pupil. He was reading Greek when only ten years old. He never entered college, but was under private tutors, at Dummer, an equivalent of two years in college.

He began life as teacher at the age of eighteen years. He taught the Feoffee's school at Ipswich with marked success, and was called to the Purchase Street school, then to the Jackman school, Newburyport. Leaving Topsfield, he was elected principal of the High school in Brattleboro, Vt., and after that service had charge of High schools in Malden, Wellesley, and Marblehead, and made an honorable record in Medford, Dedham, and Newton. One of his Topsfield students writes: "He was liked very well as a teacher; he was a very handsome man; a good penman, and taught a writing-school evenings, during the winter term." Bowdoin College conferred upon him, July 13, 1871, an honorary A. M., in recognition of his standing as a classical teacher. The honor was not sought by him, and came as a surprise.

The state of his health compelled his retirement in 1884, after a school service of more than forty years; when he returned to Newburyport, and engaged in the far less irksome duties of book-keeper and cashier for W. H. Noyes & Brother. He was prominent in church circles, and for seven years was superintendent of the "Old South" sunday school.

Mr. Noyes married, in Newbury-Byfield, Dec. 1, 1853, Miss Abby Maria Young, who was born in Newburyport, July 28, 1828, to Abigail Tenney and James Young, a grocer and trader. She died, in Newburyport, Jan. 4, 1871. He married, second, in Worcester, Dec. 29, 1874, Mary Elizabeth Moore, who was born there April 13, 1839, to Mary Fuller and Wm. G. Moore, a farmer. Prof. Noyes died Sept. 25, 1896, in his 72nd year. He had four children: twin sons, born April 26, 1857, who died less than a week old—Abbie Parish, born in Newburyport, Aug. 28, 1861; married Sept. 12, 1893, in Newburyport, Samuel Foster Jaques, a civil-engineer, who was born there, Nov. 29, 1865, to Rachel Ann Foster and Edmund Jaques, a mill-overseer; lives in Hyde Park, having one child, Mildred Noyes, born in Brockton, Sept. 29, 1895—James Young, living in Dedham, born in Newburyport, March 7, 1865; married in Dedham, Oct. 11, 1894, Ada Withington Bigelow, who was born in West Boylston, May 22, 1864, to Maria Elizabeth Fuller and Henry Clay Bigelow. Both father and son are engaged in the insurance business.

KINSMAN ATKINSON.

Rev. Kinsman Atkinson taught one term of eleven weeks in the fall of 1849. His tuition bills, written on paper $3\frac{7}{8}$ by 2 inches, are dated Nov. 12th, which was the end of the term, and show that tuition in common branches was three dollars.

Mr. Atkinson at the time was pastor of the local Methodist Episcopal Church and continued there two years. During the pastorate he also taught the Linebrook (Ipswich) winter school (1848-9) and the Topsfield North winter school (1849-50). While pastor of this church, he bought land for a parsonage; he then circulated a paper himself for funds for the house; he then collected the money and built the house; and lastly presented the parsonage to the trustees of

DANIEL OSGOOD QUINBY.

the society.   He was known as a man of great energy, quick
to discover a need and alert to supply it, and is remembered
with gratitude and great respect.

Mr. Atkinson was born at Buxton, Me., to John and Olive
(Haley) Atkinson, Oct. 16, 1807; and died at Cambridge,
Mass., Dec. 23, 1888.   He was one of twelve children; at
six years, removing with his parents to Eaton, N. H.   In
1825, he studied at Fryeburg Academy, Me.; in 1826, at
Atkinson Academy, N. H., and that year taught in Wenham.   He finished his preparation for college at Phillips
(Andover) Academy, and entered Bowdoin College in 1831;
he joined the junior class in Harvard in 1833, where he
graduated in 1834.   He studied divinity (as it used to be
called) at Andover, and Dr. Leonard Woods, professor in
the institution, paid him the high tribute: "Kinsman Atkinson is a young man of refined feelings, ardent piety, and the
best scholar in his class."   He was ordained a Congrega-
tionalist in 1838, but after five years service, changed his
views of church government and joined the M. E. church.
From 1858 to 1860, he was a supernumerary and after 1861
superannuate, when he made Cambridge his home.   His
neighbors said of him: "He always aims to do right";
others say, "We are convinced that he loved the Lord with
all his might, mind, and strength, and his neighbors as
himself."

JESSE ALLISON WILKINS.

Mr. Wilkins taught the Academy, the spring and summer
terms of 1850, teaching the Topsfield Center Grammar
school the preceding winter and the one following.

He was born at Middleton, Mass., Sept. 10, 1830, the
eighth child and fourth son in a family of thirteen children.
His parents were James Wilder and Betsey (Smith) Wilkins.
His mother was a devout Christian and helpful in church
and society.   His father was a farmer, who made home
happy, his lands productive, and was held in excellent repute among his people, so that he practiced almost every
office in their gift.   In his seventy-sixth year he was elected
to represent his district in the state legislature.

Jesse Wilkins attended the public school of his town, and

during his twelfth summer the Topsfield Academy, under
the patronage of his uncle Dr. George Sawyer, of Boxford,
who boarded him and paid his tuition. His father gave him
"his time" when he was fifteen years of age. He assumed
his middle name. His first business was an employing shoe-
maker. While thus engaged, he experienced a change of
heart, which changed his life purpose and labor.

He began to prepare for the teacher's vocation in the
spring of 1846, at the Normal Academy, Westfield. He
studied afterwards at Williston Seminary, Easthampton,
where he finished his English course. In the spring of
1851, he entered the classical department of Phillips (Andover) Academy. From that time his course was frequently
interrupted by the want of funds, and he was obliged to
have recourse to his English attainments in the practice of
archery. "Teaching the young idea how to shoot." How
long he studied at Andover is unknown to me, he was, however, a member of the junior and middle classes. The
spring and fall of 1853, he attended Phillips (Exeter)
Academy.

His first school was in Beverly, the winter of 1847-8. He
taught four grammar schools in Gloucester—two successive
winters at Riverdale, Haskell district; then the Harbor winter school; then the Point school, and afterwards the principal grammar school at the Harbor. He was next elected
to the principal school in Newbury, then to the South grammar school in Beverly, where he remained several terms—
till he resolved to relinquish the profession in 1854. In
1855, he resumed his classical studies in the private school
of Rev. Dr. Luther Wright, Easthampton, the first principal of Williston Seminary. The school was closed at the
end of his second term, and he entered the family school of
Rev Edward Root of Williamsburg, the winter of 1856.
Mr. Root accepted a call to Springfield, Ohio, and his student accepted the tuition of Rev. Dr. Gerdon Hall, Northampton. He completed his classical studies with Prof.
Calvin Stone, at Andover, during the long summer vacation
of 1857, and that fall entered Andover Theological Seminary. Owing to a protracted sickness, he did not graduate
until 1861.

He was licensed to preach by the Essex South Association of Ministers, March 5th, 1860., Dr. J. E. Dwinell, moderator. He has had four pastorates: the First Congregational Church, Hubbardston, Mass., 1861 and 2; First Congregational Church, Woodstock, Conn., 1864 and 5; the United Churches, Chesterfield, Mass., 1867 and 8; and the First Congregational Church, North Scituate, R. I., 1868 and 9.

He continued in the ministry, till the spring of 1871, when he was completely broken by nervous prostration. Repeated efforts to recuperate proved unavailing, and he sought the open air, an active pursuit, a quieter and less exacting life, and became an independent farmer. He located in Woodstock, Conn.; his health is precarious, but he is able most of the time to attend to the duties of his farm.

CHAPTER IV.

THE PERIOD OF GREATEST ACTIVITY.

GEORGE CONANT AND J. W. HEALY.

Israel Rea and Benjamin P. Adams were chiefly instrumental in the reopening of the Academy under the tuition of Mr. George Conant, in 1852. Tuition bills are extant, dated June 29, and Oct. 5, 1852, and July 7, and Oct. 5, 1853. The first term of 1853, began Jan. 19, and continued twelve weeks. Miss Lovering was preceptress in 1852, and Miss S. F. Nichols and Miss Mary Anne Friend of Georgetown in 1853.

The school prospered greatly under Mr. Conant. Its old-time reputation and activity returned. There were the Debating Club, the Young Men's League, and dramatic exhibitions, which excited great local interest and much favorable comment. The debates were participated in by the citizens as if they were students again. The interests of school and people seemed identical, and all gained pleasure and profit. Mr. Conant was apt in his management of the school, in his methods of teaching, and in his planning and conducting the public exhibitions. Miss Nichols was an accomplished scholar and belonged to a prominent family in Lowell. She was a recent graduate. Miss Lovering was much older and was employed more as a music teacher than as a teacher of general branches. Miss Friend whom he married in the fall of 1853, was daughter of John Friend and born in Andover, in 1829. She was reared in Boxford, and taught school in Georgetown. Her writings, both prose and verse "were much admired."

Miss Friend became his wife in the fall of 1853, before his last term. She taught with him about twenty-nine years, and died very suddenly in Alexandria, N. Y. After leaving Topsfield they were principal and preceptress of

(40)

Hanover Academy, Plymouth County, after which they removed to Ohio, where they taught seventeen years. He was superintendent of schools and she taught in·the High school. They afterward taught successively in Kenosha, Wis., Buffalo, N. Y., and Aurora, near Buffalo, for seven years.

Mr. Conant was born at Provincetown, Mass., May 8, 1827. His father was Rufus Conant, a merchant in Sandwich for thirty years. He was educated mainly by himself, attending an academy only a few terms. While he lived at Lyme, N. H.—a few years about 1840-45—he was a playmate with Judge C. C. Conant, now of Greenfield, Mass. By a sad accident he lost an eye when a small child. He was a fine scholar, medium height, and blue-eyed. He had a younger brother Rufus, who was of Farnsworth & Conant, lawyers, Court st., Boston, and who died March 17, 1880, leaving a widow, who now resides at Brookline.

Mr. Conant has furnished us with the following very modest yet pleasing account of himself:—

"I taught my first school in the wilds of New Hampshire, in the winter of '43 and '44· I was then between 16 and 17 years of age. Six inches of snow lay on the ground the day I opened school, Oct. 22, and it never fully left the ground during the sixteen weeks of the session. I received two dollars a week and "boarded round." The good mothers put the schoolmaster in the best room and bed, without a fire, ice and frost often sparkling in the candle-light on the walls. He thawed out the icy sheets with his warm young blood, and was ready to rise and enjoy a solid breakfast with the family before daylight. Often the snow was so deep and the distance to the school-house so great, that the big sled used for hauling wood was turned over, five or six rollicking girls and boys piled on with their well-filled dinner pails, a yoke of oxen hitched on, and with the snow up to the horned animals noses, they ploughed their slow cold way to the school-house amid the pranks and laughter of the living freight.

Fifty years afterward exactly, I visited that neighborhood, hunted for some relic of the "little red school house", but did not only fail to find some reminder of the old building, but had difficulty even in locating the site; for trees a foot in diameter stood where I a-half-century before, had "wielded

the birch." In my poem entitled "The District School of
Fifty Years Ago," I find the following lines on "Boarding
Round."

The contract with each teacher then
　　Was "so much a month and found;"
The finding in those early days
　　Was known as "Boarding Round."

How oft the "Master" wished he'd never
　　Had a calling so renowned,
Made to sit in the chimney corner,
　　A kind of oracle "Boarding Round."

Six hours labor in the school-room,
　　Ten hours in the grind-stone ground!
What a place to practice patience,
　　As he went circling, "Boarding Round."

He *must* have iron-clad "digesters,"
　　He must feelings never wound,
And be a walking cyclopedia
　　In every house, while "Boarding Round."

Obliged to smile and pet the peevish,
　　Whom 'twould have suited him to pound,
He had to flatter all the mothers,
　　Or else he couldn't "Board Around."

Called to sing when he'd be sighing,
　　And as a victim to be crowned;
Not with plaudits but with outcries,
　　"Awful nice" 'twas, "Boarding Round!"

Many a "school-marm" of that old-time,
　　Was like a pack-horse broken down,
Carrying loads by day and night-time,
　　As she plodded "Boarding Round."

Perfumed by the kitchen frying,
　　Stunned by noises as she frowned,
Frozen in the icy bed-rooms,
　　"Awful nice" 'twas, "Boarding Round!"

Yet teachers' places ne'er went begging,
Two dollars weekly, the teacher found,
No rest or surcease for the weary,
Yet awful nice 'twas, "Boarding Round!"

Before I commenced on annual school-work I had taught
five winter schools: in Lyme and Nashua, N. H.; in Marion,
Melrose, and Westport Point, Mass. The first yearly position was at Westport Point, and the second at Fall River,
Mass. Then I took charge of Topsfield Academy for two
years. Without specifying other fields of labor, I will say in
brief, I was six years as Principal in annual schools, seventeen years as superintendent of City schools, and nineteen
years as Principal of Academies.

Miss Mary Anne Friend, of Georgetown, was my last assistant in Topsfield. She became my wife in 1853 and taught
with me twenty-nine years. She was an accomplished and
thorough teacher, a writer and a poet. She excelled as a
mathematician and teacher of Latin and French. She could
shower figures on the black-board with either hand, and at
times cipher with both hands at a time, an accomplishment
seldom witnessed. She died suddenly of heart disease in
Alexandria, N. Y., Feb. 18, 1883. I have for the past five
years resided in Pasadena, California, and expect to make it
my permanent home. I gave up teaching in 1892, having
been in the school-room nearly forty-five years."

Mr. Conant is a member of the Southern California Academy of Science. He travels extensively, and is correspondent for the State Press Association of California.

JOSEPH WARREN HEALY.

J. W. Healy, A. B., succeeded Mr Conant. He began
with the summer term of 1854, and bought the property the
next following vacation. His wife, Mrs. Jane C. Healy, was
preceptress. He employed as his assistants, men of strong
character and excellent scholarship. In 1855-6 H. J. Richardson, A. B., assisted in mathematics and natural sciences; A.
J. Pike, A. B., followed him. Prof. C. P. Bronson lectured
on physiology and elocution, and Prof. A. P. Shattuck taught
penmanship. Among his assistant pupils were Daniel Wil-

kins in mathematics; A. B. Coffin and G. L. R. Gleason in vocal music; Nelson Spofford and Susan E. Perley in English branches.

Mr. Healy's first term numbered fifty scholars; the second, sixty-nine; the third, or winter (1854-5), seventy-two; the spring, one hundred and two. During 1855-6, the students numbered two hundred and three, ladies ninety-two, gentlemen one hundred and eleven; in classics fifty-two, in English one hundred and ninety-seven; summer term seventy-five, fall term one hundred, winter term ninety-eight, spring term one hundred and sixteen. It seemed as if the school had at last eaten of the tree of life and would live forever.

He revised and enlarged the course of study and adapted it to existing needs. He established two departments, Classical and English, and made "the course," three years, of four terms each. His classical course, arranged for mental discipline, led directly into New England college life. His English course provided for the needs of the business community, and embraced studies in moral science and social culture. The government was eminently parental. Tuition in common English branches was $4.00 per term, in higher English $5.00, and in the languages $1.00 each, extra.

The government is thus aptly mirrored in Mrs. Morgan's reminiscences: "Mr. Healy was quite remarkable for his punning propensity, as a mode of punishment, and woe be to the unlucky student, who received a reprimand in that way. In the lower room, desks opened with a lid, which, when raised, shielded the scholar from observation, giving a fine opportunity for cabilistic signs with fingers and face, but the 'old high desk,' reached by four steps, was the greatest torture. For some misdemeanor, the Preceptor, with the blandest smile, would request the offender to occupy the chair at his side; then while a recitation was in progress, he would draw the attention of the whole school to the recreancy, with his facetious remarks, causing a roar of merriment. Oh! what refined torture to sensitive nerves, but salutary in its effect. Government was good, and pupils were always interested in his mode of teaching, which was quite original, presenting old truths in a new dress."

REV. JOSEPH WARREN HEALY.

Every Wednesday afternoon was devoted to rhetorical exercises. Original compositions were read by the ladies, and declamations or compositions rendered by the gentlemen. Mrs. Morgan here remarks, "During those years when more than a hundred pupils responded to the roll-call, it was a trying ordeal for a young man to deliver his "maiden speech," and the ladies' presence proffered no overtures of sympathy, but rather added to his discomfiture by smiles and suppressed laughter. In the Lyceum, the tables were turned, and the gentlemen had the advantage, their laughter was outright and hearty."

The Lyceum, so popular and effective during Mr. Conant's principalship, was revived. Live questions were discussed, and it was a parliament in government. Kimball, Gleason, Wiley, Clark, Pierce, Hardy, Wilkins, Merriam, Harvey, Pearson, Towne, Porter, Rea, Balch, Stowe, Newell, Dodge, Fowler, Ames, Rollins, and others we cannot now recall, were the Websters, Clays, and Henrys of the occasion.

Besides the Lyceum, each yearly and semi-annual examination closed with an exhibition. The exhibitions were anticipated with great interest by students and citizens alike. They were planned to entertain the people. They were of high character, morally and intellectually. They were the best effort of the originators and actors. The lyceums were not alone confined to the students; citizens were invited, and many a civilian engaged in the "war of words," and many a spectator enjoyed the forensic efforts and the mirth. The practice was a strong one; it brought the two together, and a sympathy between the school and the people sprung up, of mutual benefit. Here, too, the ladies participated. If the efforts of the gentlemen were golden, the papers prepared by the ladies for the occasions were jewels in gold-settings. They were filled with solid thought, with wit and wisdom, and sparkled with merriment. They added much or most, to the enjoyment and success of the occasions.

They prepared a paper each week. Before us is a copy of the Iris and two copies of the Excelsior. Iris No. 4, says " the number of our subscribers is continually increasing"—a phrase which if original with the Iris and had been patented would have made a millionaire of the editor, for

every publisher uses it now.   One of the correspondents had
a dream, in which a stationer's show-window was exhibited
to him with ink in it that would write on any subject without
the penman's thought, except that he choose the ink adapted.   He tried some—"Sniggs' Sublime Ink"—with this result:—

THE TEMPEST CLOUD.

"Behold yon monster black as night,
On cloudy pinions swift he comes;
He rends the oak with lightning bright—
Those thorns and firey-forked tongues.
His bellowing strikes the earth with fear,
All nations tremble at the sight.
How weep the skies when he is near!
The mountains reel and rock with fright!"

The next was "Sniggs' Love Ink."

"Fair Julia, smile on me again,
Nay, do not wear that look of scorn;
Bid hope within my bosom reign,
Bid joy return and doubt begone.
Take back those cruel, cruel words
That thou so hastily hast spoken;
Let not the heart that beats for thee—
For thee alone, be rudely broken."

The Iris being a model family paper, of course had a
children's column.

CONUNDRUMS.

What street is particularly attractive to a certain young
gentleman of our school?   Bradstreet.   [Though ordinarily
a hard question, hardly a scholar could Dodge the correct
answer as given.]
Who buys algebra by the cent's worth?   S. Noyes.
Who trades in old boots and neck stocks?   Perley, Dodge,
Jenniss & Co.
The Excelsior was edited by Miss Charlotte E. Perkins.
These articles are particularly good: "Education," "The Use

of Tobacco," and "Slavery." Here are a couple of conundrums: "What young man is likely to be in great demand the coming winter? Cole (coal). A certain young lady has a warlike spirit—why? She's in favor of Killam.

Here is one of the propositions from Dorman's Moral Geometry: *Theorem*—Truth in a very low place is falsehood. First let it be admitted that all the old proverbs are true. Then submit: "Truth cannot be hid, though it lies in a well." Extending the "figure," we see that in times of great danger, a man may lie if so disposed. Q. E. D. *Corollary*—Truth is an elastic substance, from the fact that men can stretch true stories.

I am favored with an order of examination. These were usually interspersed with rhetorical exercises and occupied two or three days.

The last days of the term, May 12-13, 1856, were occupied with compositions, by Misses E. C. Batchelder, S. A. Low, M. E. Jones, M. Hale, E. A. Hood, C. Rogers, R. P. Perley, C. A. Perkins, R. E. Emerson, L. M. Bixby, C. E. Perkins, C. M. Low, E. G. Dorman, and E. A. A. Rea; and with orations by gentlemen, D. S. Balch, S. P. Fowler, C. Newell, H. B. Putnam, S. A. Merriam, H. G. Rollins, H. S. Clark, G. LeR. Gleason, and George Pierce, Jr. The subjects are not given.

The exercises in the evening were in the Congregational church and consisted of invocation, address by Rev. Mr. Dwinell, of Salem, poem by S. J. Pike, Esq., of Lawrence, which were interspersed with music by Wales' Serenade and Quadrille Band.

"Rev. Joseph Warren Healy, D. D., was born in South Hero, Vt., April 11, 1827, to Nathaniel and Jane (Tabor) Healy. He fitted for college at Newbury Seminary and Bradford Academy, Vt. He graduated at the University of Vermont in 1852. He was principal of the Bath Academy, N. H., before coming to Topsfield. While teaching at Topsfield, he supplied the pulpit of the Linebrook (Ipswich) church, perhaps two years. The Linebrook society made him a life member of the Foreign Missionary Society, April 10, 1856. The church and society under his guidance, enjoyed a period of harmony and prosperity, and grew in numbers and healthful strength. While at Topsfield he attended lectures at the Andover Theological Seminary, and was licensed by the Salem Congregational Association. Leaving the Academy, he preached at Royalston, Gardner and Walpole. Then removing to the West, he preached six years in Milwaukee, and four years in Chicago. While there he was called to the pastorate and presidency of Straight University, in New Orleans, La. There he attended medical lectures and received the medical degree. In 1871, Olivet College, Mich., conferred upon him the doctorate of divinity. He was also an LL. D.* In 1871, he was delegated by the American Missionary Association to visit Great Britain and organize an auxiliary to that society. He resided in London as its secretary for three years. While abroad, he visited the continent and the East, and lectured in the principal cities of Great Britain. Returning home he was elected professor of English literature and pastoral theology in Maryville College, Tenn. Preferring an active pastorate to the routine of professional life, he returned to Milwaukee in 1878. The death of his wife prostrated him. Subsequently he went to California for his health. In 1883, he was a pastor in Oakland, Cal. Upon the incorporation of Sierre-Madre College, at Pasadena, in 1884, he was selected as the president. Subsequent to 1885, he retired from the ministry, resided in San Diego, Cal., and latterly practised medicine."

*For the purpose of the General Catalogue of his *Alma Mater*, it was thought necessary to know the source and date of his title LL. D., and the date of his title M. D. About twenty-five communications are before me relative to its source and their dates. They all rest upon memory, and agree wonderfully in regard to the time, yes, and source also. The words of Gen. Chas. H. Howard and Rev. E. M. Strieby, D. D., who were quite familiar with his work in New Orleans, are as pertinent as any.

Gen. Howard says:

"My impression is strong that the title LL. D., was given Dr. Healy by Straight University, at the time of his going to Europe." Later he wrote:—"I remember that Dr. Healy had the degree conferred upon him, about the time he went abroad to reside in London, and that is about all I know concerning the matter."

Dr. Strieby writes:

"The vague impression on my mind is that he obtained this degree, with several other honorary titles, such as F. R. S., etc., in Great Britain. Of this I am not sure. It is barely possible they may have been given to him by the S. U." * * * * "Yet, I fear that nothing will be found, for our people were then engaged in making history and not in writing it."

Mr. Healy was a diligent worker, an excellent teacher, social, genial, a ready reader of human nature, and easily made himself master. He led his school; his scholars were ambitious, diligent, social, and in the main made the most of their opportunities. He was ambitious. In whatever he engaged, he threw his entire self. Whatever he did, was well done, from principle. Every station he held he made an opening door to the next higher station. He used to say to his scholars: "Be not bent by circumstances, but bend them."* He loved to do good, realizing that in such service was his highest honor. That idea was the inspiration of his life; and his life subserved that great end.

While preaching at Linebrook, he took one and another of his older students with him, to the religious meetings of the parish, thus introducing them into society and its service, and giving a practical turn to school life. We know of his saying "Come into the school and if the burden of the tuition is too great, it will be remitted." Whatever was money in his family was good for tuition, and many a farmer-lad thus figured out results to a fraction. Among his students, he was a whole "Lend-a-Hand" Society, judicious and efficient.

After leaving the Academy, but before going west, he united the society of Royalston, paid their church debt and repaired the church. At Walpole he enlarged the sphere and usefulness of the church and society, and solidified its strength. He was at Gardner, a preacher they praised. Coming out of the church edifice one Sunday, we heard— "That was an able discourse"—"yes, it was; I never heard that subject handled better." His society was proud of him.

In the west, he was the same scholarly, eloquent helper. In Chicago he was, under God, the organizer of twelve religious societies that built church edifices. But more, he would herald the truth from pulpit and press. He was one of the founders of *The Advance*, a paper of high rank and doctrinal authority.

---

*Circumstances, on occasions, seemed to be made for him, or required but little bending. Upon hearing a rumor of Mr. Healy's death, the writer sent a missive of inquiry into his vicinity. The letter fell into his hand, when he immediately sent "a penny messenger" on which was written: "Psalm 118, vs. 18 and 17. As ever thine. J. W. H."

In New Orleans, he was pastor of the First Congregational Church, and was consulted for "the benefit of his judgment in selecting points in Louisiana, for schools." During the year 1869-70, he was president of Straight University, and superintendent of church organization for Louisiana, Mississippi, and Texas. The next two years he was president, three years in all, but was absent in Great Britain, soliciting funds for scholarships. This was his work for the A. M. A., the patron of the University.

The test of establishing churches and schools in the South, just following the War of the Rebellion, was as exacting as it was noble. It required judgment and knowledge pre-eminent, tact and discretion, and, withall, a readiness of heart and hand. It was a place of dignity, learning and religious character. Mr. Healy's part was done acceptably, promptly and honorably. So well and favorably was he known and appreciated among the literati, that there was power in the mention of his name.

Rev. D. W. Hanna, president of Los Angeles College, says of Sierra-Madre College, Pasadena, of which Dr. Healy was president:—"A liberal grant was made for it, a good school building was erected, and the site was admirable; but Pasadena did not prove attractive—it seemed impossible to awaken adequate enthusiasm. The school numbered from thirty to fifty students. It was started under the leadership of Rev. J. W. Ellis, D. D., of San Francisco. Shortly after the college opened, the board of trustees elected Dr. Healy, who was then pastor of the Presbyterian Church, at Santa Monica, to the presidency, *for the influence of his name.* Dr. Healy's health was then very poor, and he did not occupy the office, nor change his residence, nor take any active part in the college work. He resigned at the end of his year, 1884-5, and Prof. J. M. Coyner presided. The doctor was in no way responsible for the college. It continued about two years; the building is now a private residence." Mr. Hanna spoke very highly of Dr. Healy's work at Santa Monica.

He married, Oct. 8, 1848, Miss Jane Hibbard Clark, who was born in Groton, Vt., May 12, 1830. She studied in the Female Seminary, Burlington, Vt., taught with her husband at Bath and Topsfield, and adorned the place of a pastor's wife wherever he labored. She died at her mother's home in Corinth, Vt., Sept. 12, 1880, beloved and lamented, a pure and gentle spirit. Their children were Jane Corinne, who was born March 6, 1850, and died October 8, 1850; and Frank Joseph, who was born March 4, 1857; studied at Olivet College and London (England) University; was admitted to the bar, 1878; was editor of the Gazette, Fort Wayne, Ind., till 1884; and is now on the editorial staff of the Tribune, Cleveland, O.

His second wife was Mrs. Ellen R. White, widow of W. M. White, a merchant of Washington, D. C., who died there of consumption. She was Miss Young, born in Bangor, Me., Feb. 2, 1833. She became Mrs. Healy July 21, 1884, while he was preaching in Santa Monica. She has built her a home at Riverside, Cal., but will spend her summers at San Diego.

Mr. Healy preached about three years in Woodland, and Oakland, before visiting southern California. He was pastor of the Presbyterian church at Santa Monica, three years. He never recovered from the prostration following his first wife's death. He loved life and labor, and when driven by ill health from one field, he sought another field immediately upon recuperation. As a last resort, when he could no longer stand to preach, in the fall of 1886, he sought a change of air and began to practise medicine in San Diego. He died of spinal abscess, April 26, 1887, and was buried at San Diego, under imposing and solemn rites by Masons and Odd Fellows. He was paralyzed and speechless for 20 hours, a patient sufferer. Dr. Healy was an exemplary man—one of nature's noblemen. He arose by his own exertions, and achieved a grand success. His titles are emblems of his character and attainments.

The Congregational Year Book says:—"Mr. Henry Jackson Richardson was born in Middleton, Mass., June 23, 1829, to Daniel and Olive Berry (Perkins) Richardson. He fitted for college at Phillips Academy, and graduated at Amherst, in 1855, and at Andover Theological Seminary, in 1859; taught in the Topsfield Academy, 1855-6, was ordained at Lincoln, Mass., Sept. 6, 1860; and was released from active

pastoral charge, May 10, 1892.   He married, June 26, 1864,
Mrs. Harriet Amelia, widow of Theodore French, of Con-
cord, N. H., and daughter of Dea. William and Abby (Reed)
Colburn, of Lincoln.   He died of la grippe, Dec. 19, 1893."

Rev. Alpheus Justus Pike, who was assistant to Profs.
Healy and Allis, was born in Topsfield, March 7, 1828.   His
father was a farmer and cultivated broad fields and rich soil.
He was educated at Thetford Academy, Vt., and at Dart-
mouth College, graduating in 1855.   He studied theology at
Andover, Mass., and at East Windsor, now Hartford, Conn.
He was ordained and installed at Marlboro, Conn., and after-
wards had successive charge of churches in Sauk Centre,
Minn., and Mandan and Dawson, Dak.   He has also labored
for the American Missionary Association both in the United
States and Great Britain.   He is now located at Dwight,
Dakota.

Mrs. Morgan says:—"Our respected teacher and townsman
A. J. Pike, A. B., afterwards a minister, is well remembered.
He was a most thorough scholar; he always carried the text
books closed in his hand without the slightest thought of re-
ferring to them.   In the clear, autumn evenings, he would
take the class out on the hills and point out the different constellations, making our lessons in astronomy of practical
value."

Prof. B. Robert Downes, Bradford, was a teacher of music
during Prof. Healy's principalship and those who followed.
His only business was teaching music, chiefly, it is understood, instrumental.   He was always busy—"have all I can
do," as he once remarked.   Here Mrs. Morgan remarks:—
"I must not forget Professor of music, B. R. Downes.   Can
we not see him passing from home to home of his pupils,
swinging his cane in the air, ready to fall in repeated blows
on reaching the door, then taking quiet little naps while the
lessons were thrummed, always good-natured and happy."

CHAPTER V.

————

Prof. O. D. Allis, A. M., began here with the winter term of 1856-7, and closed his services with the fall term of 1858. He continued the school in relation to the course of study, terms and tuition, as these had been adopted by Mr. Healy. The character of the school was fully sustained. A. J. Pike, A. B., assisted him in the winter term; Austin Hazen, A. B., in the spring term; L. T. Burbank, A. B., of Williams College, thereafter. Mrs. Mary A. Jones was preceptress, Miss C. M. Thurston was assistant. Prof. B. R. Downes, jr., taught piano music; G. LeR. Gleason, vocal music; and Daniel T. Ames, penmanship.

Three rhetorical programs have been loaned me. May 6, 1857, has the following orations:—Every man a debtor to his profession, by George L. Blanchard; Influence of Washington, by M. V. B. Perley; The present crisis of our country, by D. F. Towne; Athens, by S. A. Merriam; The scholar's hope, by J. G. Colt; The mind measured by its object, by G. E. Joslin; Decay an element of growth, by D. T. Ames; The influence of the age in producing great men, by G. LeR. Gleason; Eloquence of decay, by N. T. Kimball; Israel Putnam, by S. P. Fowler. Compositions were read by Misses L. Burbank, S. A. Chamberlain, H. McLoud, M. A. Hoyt, H. A. Wells, E. A. R. Towne, E. A. Putnam, H. M. Kimball, M. M. Farrar, C. F. Kimball, M. A. Dickinson, R. P. Perley, C. A. Perkins, C. E. Batchelder, and A. Rogers.

The rhetorical exercises, Nov. 11, 1857, were:—Orations— Ambition essential to great achievements, by Geo. F. Flint; Responsibility of Americans, by J. C. Leonard; The Press, by N. D. Dodge; The condition and prospects of America, by

(53)

C. A. Mooar; Arnold, the traitor, by M. H. Dorman; John Q. Adams, by J. W. Porter; Dr. Kane, by C. Fowler; Revolutions, by J. K. Cole; Earth's benefactors, by M. V. B. Perley; Earth's malefactors, by Geo. L. Blanchard; Skepticism, by D. T. Ames. The following had compositions:—Misses S. A. Chamberlin, J. K. Noyes, S. M. Ray, M. M. Thompson, M. A. Hoyt, H. E. Peabody, C. A. Berry, C. C. Peabody, M. E. Choate, R. P. Balch, R. P. Perley, E. B. Perley, A. P. Kimball, C. W. Woodbury. The program concluded with a colloquy, "Home Government," written by the students—Misses M. Low, L. D. Hardy and M. A. C. Noyes.

The rhetorical program of Nov. 10, 1858, was:—Declamation, by Hamilton Temple; Orations—Dr. Livingstone, by A. M. Merriam; Object of our mission, by J. W. Perkins; The power of knowledge, by N. D. Dodge, jr.; Enthusiasm, by C. A. Mooar; Jephtha's daughter, by Geo. F. Flint; The nobility and responsibility of the teacher's vocation, by J. K. Cole; Reform, by Clarence Fowler; Moral force the only instrument of freedom, by M. V. B. Perley; Young America, by H. G. Rollins; and the reading of the school paper, "*The Laural Wreath*," by Misses Abbie R. Cole and Rebecca K. Bixby, Clarence Fowler, editor.

These exercises were always interspersed with music, generally by a hired orchestra, sometimes by the school talent.

Prof. Allis came to Topsfield with an experience of some seven or eight years. He was a good teacher and disciplinarian. His want of health was the only impediment to good rank among noted teachers. He was tall and slim; his configuration and movements betokened insidious disease. He had a deep voice and was an excellent bass singer. His voice was cultured and he excelled as a reader. He was a good scholar, critical in the recitation and apt in his illustrations. His manner was pleasing; his conversation, entertaining; his social life, unblamable; and remembrance of him is pleasant indeed.

Mr. Allis was born in Brookfield, Vt., July 27, 1825, to Elisha and Mary (Steele) Allis. While at home he attended the district school and the academy at Randolph. His preparation for college was completed at Thetford Academy. He entered Williams College, and during this second year returned home sick, where he remained an invalid for a year. He received the honorary degree of A. M., from the University of Vermont. He taught a year in Barre Academy, under J. S. Spaulding; then at Vergennes some two or three years. While at Vergennes he married Miss Ann Eliza Colt, of Brookfield. Subsequently he taught at Chelsea perhaps four or five years; then at Topsfield. From here he went to Randolph Centre, Vt., where he preached three or four years; thence to West Randolph where he preached about five years. The state of his health was to him, all the while, a source of anxiety and expense, and an impediment in his work. At last his active life closed; in 1866 he repaired to Danielsonville, N. Y., for treatment at that noted water-cure. He died there in June, 1867, nearly forty-two years old. His disease was chronic rheumatism, culminating in congestion of the lungs. He was buried in West Randolph. Thus perished an active life, a generous heart, a noble purpose, a Christian man.

The Lyceum, so popular with Principal Conant's and Principal Healy's schools, was fully sustained during Mr. Allis' principalship. Citizens participated in and enjoyed the occasions. The students regarded it a part of their school life, and prepared for it, in the main, as for a recitation, or the weekly rhetorical exercises.

The first Lyceum of which we have any record was organized on Dec. 24, 1856. The members were J. Brown, J. Pike, A. M. Trask, E. W. Pert, A. E. Baker, T. F. Towne, J. E. Leonard, M. H. Dorman, M. V. B. Perley, C. M. Boyd, J. W. Porter, J. G. Colt, Geo. L. Blanchard, A. D. Pearson, W. T. McQuestion and James Ingalls.

Prof. Allis, principal of the school called the meeting to order. Towne was voted president, pro tem.; Colt, secretary, pro tem. Brown, Blanchard, Dorman, committee to draft constitution and by-laws. Dec. 31. Blanchard was voted president, pro tem.; Colt secretary, pro tem.; constitution and by-laws adopted. The former authorized primarious, president, vice-president, secretary; the latter, this order of business: reading minutes of last meeting, declamations, discussions, miscellaneous business, reading of school-paper, appointment of editors, readers, and judges of discussions as to force of argument.

The principal was primarius and embodied all final authority.   Teachers were ex-officio members, and lady-students
at their option.   Male members signed constitution and by-
laws and paid the bills, (perhaps 25 cents per term.)   Jan.
7, 1857.   Blanchard and Colt were voted again pro tem.
Constitutional officers by ballot: Boyd, president; M. V. B.
Perley, vice-president; Colt, secretary.   Boyd and Joslin,
affirmative, and Towne and Colt, negative, discussed "Is a
nation justified in rising against its rulers?" and the judges
gave the better argument to the affirmative.   Jan. 14.   Brown
and Towne, affirmative, and Blanchard and Leonard, negative, discussed "Does wealth exert a greater influence than
education?" which was decided in the affirmative.   Jan. 28.
Towne and Joslin, affirmative, and A. D. Pearson and J. E.
Pike, negative: "Are railroads an advantage or disadvant-
age to a country?"   The affirmative won.

Spring term, 1857.   March 11.   Members: D. T. Ames, G.
A. Ames, J. C. Colt, J. W. Porter, G. L. Blanchard, S. P.
Fowler, jr., C. M. Boyd, A. D. Pearson, G. E. Joslin, S. A.
Merriam, N. T. Kimball, M. V. B. Perley.   D. T. Ames was
voted president; S. P. Fowler, jr., vice-president; G. E. Joslin, secretary.   Pearson declaimed.   Kimball and Fowler,
affirmative, and Porter and Perley, negative: "Resolved, that
the mariner's compass has been more beneficial to man than
the printing press."   Negative won.   March 16.   Blanchard
and Perley declaimed.   Fowler and Boyd, affirmative, and
Gleason and Colt, negative: "Is a man the arbiter of his own
fortune?"   Affirmative won.   Misses Batchelder and Perley
read "The Iris," A. D. Pearson, editor.   March 23.   Colt and
Gleason declaimed.   Porter and Joslin, affirmative, and G.
A. Ames and Towne, negative: "Was Washington a greater
man than Columbus?"   Affirmative won.   March 30.   Pearson declaimed.   Blanchard and D. T. Ames, affirmative, and
Merriam and Gleason, negative: "Should non-intervention
be the policy of the U. S.?"   Affirmative prevailed.   Misses
Thurston and Rogers read "The Iris," G. A. Ames, editor.
April 6.   Perley and Joslin declaimed.   Fowler and Towne,
affirmative, and Kimball and Porter, negative: "Should the
sale of intoxicating liquors be prohibited by law?"   April
13.   G. A. Ames and Gleason, affirmative, and H. O. Wiley,

negative: "Is the progress of the present age greater than
that of past ages?" Affirmative won. Misses E. F. and H.
M. Kimball read "The Iris," Gleason, editor. April 20.
Kimball and Porter, affirmative, and Joslin and Towne, nega-
tive: "Is ambition the cause of more good than evil?"
Misses Chamberlain and Farrar read "The Iris." April 27.
Fowler and Long declaimed. Porter and Kimball, affirma-
tive, and Gleason and D. T. Ames, negative: "Is a republi-
can form of government more stable than a monarchial one?"
Misses Wells and Towne read "The Iris," Perley, editor.

Winter term, 1857-8. Dec. 3. Members: J. W. Porter,
D. F. Towne, M. H. Dorman, W. L. Putnam, G. H. Peabody,
A. F. Smith, A. A. Fowler, C. W. Peart, J. N. Smith, S. T.
J. Byam, L. W. Green, W. S. Merrill, B. A. Shute, P. S.
Farnsworth, J. A. Friend, G. D. Richards, C. Porter, J. R.
Jackson, Jos. Ridgway, E. F. Esty, H. Temple, M. A. Kent,
L. L. Robbins, E. F. Creesy, A. M. Merriam, H. L. Long, J.
H. Towne, S. Fuller, J. C. Bancroft, D. G. Upton, N. A. Pike,
J. Swinerton, W. H. Preston, W. P. Hutchinson, S. Noyes.
J. W. Porter was voted president, pro tem.; Dorman, secre-
tary, pro tem.; Dorman, D. F. Towne, W. L. Putnam, a
committee on constitution and by-laws. Dec. 9, constitution
and by-laws were adopted. J. W. Porter was voted president; D. F. Towne, vice-president; M. H. Dorman, secretary. Dec. 16. Dorman and Shute declaimed. Putnam
and Green, affirmative, and Dorman and Noyes, negative:
"Is a skillful politician better fitted for a president of the U. S.
than a skillful general?" Affirmative was victor. Dec. 23.
Jackson and J. W. Porter declaimed. J. W. Porter and Farnsworth, affirmative, and Ridgway and Peabody, negative: "Is
the fear of punishment a greater incentive to exertion than the
hope of reward?" Valorous, affirmative! Misses Peabody
and A. P. Kimball read "The Iris," Dorman, editor. Dec.
30. Town and Shute declaimed. W. L. Putnam and Robbins,
affirmative, and Noyes and Jackson, negative: "Does the
constitution of these U. S. conflict with American slavery?"
Valorous, negative! Jan. 6. Farnsworth and Dorman declaimed. S. Fuller and A. F. Smith, affirmative, and Dorman and Ridgway, negative: "Is a republican government
better to live under than a monarchy?" Negative won.

Jan. 13, 1858. Friend, Putnam, C. Porter declaimed. Pope and Dorman, affirmative, and D. F. Towne and W. L. Putnam, negative: "Is novel reading deleterious to the public mind?" Jan. 27. C. Porter and Putnam declaimed. Ridgway and Dorman, affirmative, and Swinerton and W. L. Putnam, negative: "Is man the arbiter of his own fortune?" Negative won. Misses Woodbury and Low read "The Iris," Pope, editor. Feb. 10. Farnsworth, Green, J. W. Porter, Temple, Dorman declaimed. Pope and C. Porter, affirmative, and J. W. Porter and Temple negative: "Has science accomplished more than physical strength?" Affirmative won. Misses Thurston and E. F. Kimball read "The Iris," D. F. Towne, editor.

Spring term, 1858. Feb. 22. Members: D. F. Ames, C. A. Mooar, Geo. L. Blanchard, L. L. Robbins, H. Temple, J. Ridgway, J. R. Jackson, Asbury Osgood, Myron R. Hutchinson, J. E. Leonard, J. C. Lavalette, J. K. Cole, N. D. Dodge, B. Alward Shute, J. Wright Perkins, S. Noyes, M. V. B. Perley. D. T. Ames was voted moderator, pro tem.; C. Fowler, secretary, pro tem.; and D. F. Towne, Perley, C. Fowler, a committee on constitution and by-laws. Blanchard was chosen editor of "The Iris." J. K. Cole and J. E. Leonard were chosen president and vice-president for one week. March 1. Constitution and by-laws were adopted. C. Fowler and Leonard, affirmative, and N. D. Dodge and Mooar, negative: "Is the pen mightier than the sword?" Affirmative won. Misses Kimball and Towne read "The Iris," Blanchard, editor. Permanent officers: Ridgway, secretary; J. K. Cole, president; G. L. Blanchard, vice-president. March 8. Meech and Mooar declaimed. Blanchard and D. T. Ames, affirmative, and C. Fowler and Jackson, negative: "Which exerts the greater influence in the world, man or woman?" Affirmative won. Misses Noyes read "The Iris." March 15. Blanchard and Lavalette declaimed. Leonard and D. T. Ames, affirmative, and Dodge and Cole, negative: "Are the works of nature more admired than the works of art?" Affirmative carried the argument. Misses Cole and Lamson read "The Iris." March 22. Leonard and Jackson declaimed. Perley and Ridgway, affirmative, and Robbins and A. H. Meech, negative: "Does wealth exert a greater influence than education?" Affirmative won. Misses Cushing and Perkins read "The Iris." March 29. Temple and Hutchinson declaimed. Noyes and Mooar, affirmative, and Lavalette and Jackson, negative: "Has the mariner's compass been of more benefit to man than the printing-press?" Negative won. April 5. J. W. Perkins and D. T. Ames, affirmative, and Blanchard and ———, negative: "Are political parties beneficial to a State?" Affirmative conquered. "The Iris" was postponed and Henry G. Rollins, of Groveland, lectured on "The intelligent and enterprising American." April 12. Perkins and Cole declaimed. Cole and J. W. Porter, affirmative, and Ridgway and Leonard, negative: "Was Wellington a greater man than Bonaparte?" Affirmative won. Misses Adams and Ober read "The Iris," Cole, editor.

(Several pages are here missing.)

Fall term, 1859. Sept. 11. Members: Hamilton Temple, Bartlett H. Weston, Geo. E. Weaver, J. Welch Porter, Edward B. Putnam, J. W. Perkins, Wm. H. Dalton. Porter was voted president; Temple, scribe; Geo. T. Welch, vice-president. Appointments: Geo. E. Warner, to declaim; Perkins, affirmative, and Weston, negative: "Should we obey a law which we think to be morally wrong?" Minnie L. Putnam and Hattie Dorman, readers, and Welch, editor. Sept. 21. Warner declaimed; Perkins and Weston discussed, and "judged in the negative." Oct. 5. John W. Porter and E. B. Putnam declaimed. Warner, affirmative, and Welch, negative: "Is the mind of woman inferior to that of man?" Negative had the argument. Misses Hattie Dorman and Minnie L. Putnam read "The Topsfield News," Welch, editor. Oct. 12. Misses Reed and Weston read "The News," Flint, editor. Edward E. Putnam was tried for and found guilty of the murder of Sparticus. He was sentenced to be hanged by the arms till the rope broke "The execution occupied just one second." Oct. 19. Misses Fairfield and Eaton read "The News," Perkins, editor. Perkins, affirmative, and Porter, negative: "Is the hope of reward a greater incentive than the fear of punishment?" Nov. 2. Otis F. Dodge, affirmative, and Geo. E. Nichols, negative: "Re-

solved, that wealth exerts a greater influence than education?"
Affirmative won.   Misses Howe and Fairfield read "The
Laural Wreath," J. W. Perkins, editor.

Spring term, 1860.   Feb. 29.   Constitution of 1856 was
adopted.   J. Adams was chosen president; Jos. P. Wonson,
secretary.   March 7.   "An eloquent discussion:"—J. W.
Perkins, B. Weston, Otis F. Dodge, affirmative, and ———
Gen.———Cole, J. P. Wonson, negative: "Resolved, that the
so-called strikes now being made by the shoemakers of surrounding towns will be a benefit?"   Otis F. Dodge was
chosen president; John W. Perkins, vice-president; Jos. P.
Wonson, secretary.

Mrs. Mary Amanda Jones, preceptress, was educated at
Newbury Seminary, Vermont.   She came to this school a
talented and finely educated teacher.   Her gentle manners
and kindly disposition won the respect of all, and the love of
those in her immediate care.   She was tall, and a lady of
commanding figure, which, supplemented by her gentle manners, gave her a presence remarkably suggestive of Virgil's
"quæ incedo regina."   She remained with the school till the
close of the year 1858-9.

Mrs. Jones was born in Sutton, Vt., July 5, 1830, to Phoebe
Fletcher and Rev. Elisha Brown.   She married, Oct. 20, 1852,
Edwin Alonzo Jones, M. D., and two years later was left a
widow.   For twelve years thereafter she was engaged in
teaching in public schools and high-grade seminaries, at
Springfield, Vt., Amenia, N. Y., Topsfield and Auburndale,
Mass.

After leaving Auburndale, she married, in Berlin, Vt.,
July 22, 1866, Rev. Rodney Howland Howard, D. D., of the
N. E. Conference, and pastor of the M. E. Church, in Mon-
son, Mass.   She died in Franklin, Mass., April 12, 1892.

Dr. Howard married, second, Mrs. Susan Cheney Jones,
widow of Loren Washburn Jones, merchant, West Somer-
ville, and daughter of Adolphus and Susan (Tenney) Tenney,
undertaker and dealer in furniture, Windsor, Vt.   Dr. Howard died Jan. 3, 1897.

Lysander T. Burbank was an assistant to Mr. Allis during
the summer term of 1857.

Mr. Burbank was born in Fitzwilliam, N. H., Nov. 24,

MR. AND MRS. AUSTIN HAZEN.

1828, to John and Hannah (Lyon) Burbank. His father was a farmer. He graduated at Williams College, 1857, and at Union Theological Seminary, New York City, 1860. He married Sarah Susannah Van Vlack of New York City, and in July of the same year he sailed from Boston under appointment as missionaries of the A. B. C. F. M., to Turkey, on the barque Smyrniote, for Smyrna, laden with a cargo of New England rum, and missionaries as passengers, arriving at Bitlis in Oct., 1860. They gave up their foreign work finally on account of ill-health, and returned to America in 1870. The work in Turkey resulted in establishing several flourishing churches and schools, and in training young men and women for teachers and preachers, and correlative labor. He says, "it was the greatest trial of my life to leave that blessed work." In his preparation for the work he attended a course of medical lectures in New York City, and also dispensary practice, receiving "A Certificate of Honor," conferring the title of Dr.

He became pastor of a church in Herndon, Va., in 1871; removing in 1880 to Georgetown, Neb., to become pastor of the Burr Oak Presbyterian church. He was there in 1890.

They have (1890) six children living. One reposes in Bitlis, dying Jan., 1864; another in Herndon, dying July, 1874. Their oldest, Frederic L., is an M. D., and practicing in Hooper, Neb., and the oldest daughter, Mary S., married David Montgomery, a graduate of Hastings College and engaged in Y. M. C. A. work, but hoping to go a missionary to China.

Austin Hazen, Prof. Allis's assistant, was born in Hartford, Vt., Feb. 14, 1835, to Rev. Austin and Lucia (Washburn) Hazen. He went with his father's family to Berlin, at the age of three years. He fitted for college at home and at St. Johnsbury Academy, graduating at the University of Vermont, Burlington, in 1855. Taught one year in Barre Academy, and graduated at the Theological Seminary, Andover, Mass., in 1859. During his first year at Andover he taught the spring term of the Topsfield Academy. Mr. Allis was an invalid and the work of the principal came mostly upon Mr. Hazen. After graduation, he preached at Norwich, Vt., from 1859 to 1864; then at Jericho Centre, Vt., from 1864

to 1884. He began to preach also in Richmond, Vt., in 1875.
In 1884, he removed to Richmond, where he completed his
life work. He was two years superintendent of schools in
Norwich, and two in Jericho. His sickness was long and
painful, and though accompanied by severe sufferings caused
by repeated attempts of the surgeons to bring relief, he
uttered no word of complaint. He died May 22, 1895, while
on a passage to Europe, and was buried at sea, in the bosom
of "old gray ocean."

He married Feb. 12, 1862, Mary Jane Carleton, who was
born in October, 1840, to Mary Wheeler and David Carleton, a farmer, of Barre, Vt. She died April 18, 1880, in Jericho Centre. He married, 2nd, in Keeseville, N. Y., June 1,
1881, Almira Farrington Elliot, who was born Feb. 21, 1838,
to Eliza Hall and Ezra Elliot, a farmer, of Croydon, N. H.

His first wife was mother of all his children, seven sons
and one daughter, Mary Carleton, who was born July 20,
1875, and died the next January. The seven sons have
graduated in the course in arts at the University of Vermont.
Four have graduated from the Hartford, Ct., Theological
Seminary and are in the Congregational ministry. Austin,
born Sept. 20, 1863, who received the seminary fellowship
for two years' study in Germany, 1893 to 1895; Carleton,
born June 14, 1865; Frank William, born Jan. 7, 1869, and
William, born Nov. 3, 1870. Two are physicians. Allen,
born May 12, 1867, a graduate of the College of Physicians
and Surgeons of New York, and Robert, born Dec. 2, 1872,
a graduate in medicine at the University of Vermont; and
Tracy, born July 4, 1874, will complete his post-graduate
studies in science, at Columbia College, 1899. This is a remarkable family in its obvious aspect. The father is working now in the field ready for harvest with seven-fold opportunity and power.

At college, his scholarship ranked with the best; at the
seminary, he was one of the best Hebraists; as a minister,
"he kept his science of religion properly in the background,
but his instructions and counsels were never inconsistent with
the logical framework which underlay all his thinking;" as a
man, his scholarship, his utterances, his amiableness and demeanor were hardly noticed in their individuality. In this

regard he was peculiar; the traits of his character were most happily blended, no one was unduly prominent, each seemed designed to perfect the rest; his character was a constellation, like the sweet influence of the Pleiades, and cultivated friendship, molded character, inculcated principle, inspired love; and because the influence was all unconscious to giver and receiver, it was the more potent. His life though humble was forceful, and though it was circumscribed in action, it was unbounded in influence.

Charles Morgan Pierce, assisted Mr. Allis in 1857-8. He says, "Mr. Allis was the principal, but owing to his illness the school for the greater part of the year was in my hands."

Mr. Pierce was born Oct. 18, 1834, to Erastus and Sophia (Morgan) Pierce, in Hinsdale, Mass. He studied at Hinsdale Academy and graduated at Williams College in 1857. He taught in the Academy one year, 1857-8, and by reason of Mr. Allis' feeble health, sustained the burden of the school. He entered Andover Seminary with the junior class of 1858, and remained two years, when he was appointed instructor in mathematics and Latin at his Alma Mater, a position he held two years. He was licensed to preach by the Berkshire Northern Association, Oct. 29, 1860. He supplied the Congregational Church in Peru six months of 1862. He became a resident student at Andover, Oct., 1862, and became the stated supply of the West Boxford church, where he was ordained and installed Sept. 2, 1863. He was dismissed July 17, 1867, and the next September accepted the *pro tempore* professorship of mathematics in Williams College, which he held till April, 1868, supplying the while the Congregational Church at South Williamstown. He was installed at Middlefield, Mass., July 1, 1868, and resigning on account of ill-health, was dismissed July 26, 1881. He was acting pastor at Charlton, from Aug. 20, 1882, to Dec. 6, 1885; was pastor at Hardwick, from Dec. 13, 1885, to April 1, 1890, when he resigned to accept a pastorate in Auburn, where he now resides. He has published two funeral discourses, 1864, 1873.

He married in Salem, Mass., Aug. 12, 1863, Elizabeth Morse Peabody. They have one child, Charles Peabody, born Oct. 19, 1869, who is now of the class of '92 academical department, Yale University.

The following pertinent comment is by Mrs. Morgan: "Charles H. Pierce taught a year or more, as preceptor for Mr. Allis, who was in feeble health. Mr. Pierce won the esteem of all his pupils by his uniform kindness and patience. He came as an assistant and rather shrank from full charge of the school, which the Principal's illness made necessary; still his thorough knowledge of all the branches taught, and easy manners and fluent speaking, made him a very popular teacher."

"An old friend of education" wrote thus of the school for the *Salem Gazette*, in 1857:—

TOPSFIELD ACADEMY.—The Semi-Annual Examination of this successful Institution, was on Wednesday, July 15th. The writer had the pleasure of being present in the afternoon, and was highly interested. The exercises commenced with singing by the members of the school, which convinced all that there was no lack of musical talent. Declamations were then given by J. H. Byne, of Galveston, Texas; M. V. B. Perley, of Ipswich; and A. D. Pearson, of Topsfield; all of whom did credit to themselves and the school.

The Orations, with the subjects, were as follows:—The Love of Liberty, George P. Flint, North Reading; Struggles, Jefferson K. Cole, Boxford; Death, Clarence Fowler, Danvers; Mental Culture, Daniel F. Ames, Vershire, Vt.; Influence of Great Men on their Age, Henry G. Rollins, Georgetown. The Orations were creditable to their writers and the school. The last one, by H. G. Rollins, would compare favorably with the best productions of College graduates, and do honor to many men of high pretentions. Next came the reading of the paper, published by the school. The Editor, H. G. Rollins, introduced Miss Abbie Cole, of Topsfield, and Miss Mary Cushing, of Williamstown, as the *readers*, who interested those present, for the space of half an hour, with rich gems of thought and wit, causing many a hearty laugh.

We next listened to the reading of essays by the following ladies of the graduating class:—Cornelia M. Thurston, of Vershire, Vt.; Margaret A. Hoyt, Georgetown; Charlotte A. Perkins and Ellen F. Kimball, of Topsfield. The essays were finely written and very pleasing. The one by Miss

Kimball, on the Marriage of the Hemispheres, was particularly good, being written in an easy, natural style, and well read.

At the close of the exercises, Diplomas were presented to those graduating, with appropriate remarks, by the worthy and able Principal, O. D. Allis, A. M.

Topsfield Academy has a fine location, and we were happy to find the school in such a flourishing condition. Although we were told by the Principal that the past term had not been so fully attended as previous terms, yet the school was in a healthy and promising state, and as long as its present Board of Teachers remain, we have high hopes of its success.

"A friend to education" chronicled the following of the Academy in Nov., 1858:—It was our good fortune, two days last week, to attend the quarterly examination of the Topsfield Academy, and it was very pleasant for us to witness the appearance of success, which crowned the labor of the teachers and students. The degree of proficiency exhibited by the classes in Greek, Latin and French, was highly creditable, but the rhetorical Exercise, which was during the afternoon of Wednesday, was particularly interesting. The exercise consisted of Orations from a large part of the gentlemen, and the reading of the Laurel Wreath, a literary journal consisting mostly of compositions from the ladies of the Institution. The order of the exercises was as follows:—

Orations were delivered by A. M. Merriam, subject, "Dr. Livingstone;" J. W. Perkins, subject, "Objects of our Mission;" N. D. Dodge, Jr., subject, "The Power of Knowledge;" C. A. Mooar, subject, "Enthusiasm;" G. F. Flint, subject, "Jephtha's Daughter;" J. K. Cole, subject, "The Nobility and Responsibility of the Teacher's Vocation;" Clarence Fowler, subject, "Reform;" M. V. B. Perley, subject, "Moral Force the only Instrument of Freedom;" H. G. Rollins, subject, "Young America." Music, of a high order, was listened to, consisting of pieces sung by a select choir, between the delivery of the Orations. After the speaking, the "Laurel Wreath," edited by Clarence Fowler, was read by the Editresses, Miss Abbie R. Cole, and Miss Rebecca K. Bixby. The contributions to the paper displayed marked talent, and were highly creditable to the ladies. The style in which the orations were written, and delivered, showed that the gentlemen had talent, which might be profitably cultivated. The one entitled "Jephtha's Daughter," was spoken in such a manner, that we could almost seem to see the Maiden kneeling before the Chief of Israel, to receive her death-blow; and another entitled, "The Nobility and Responsibility of the Teacher's Vocation," contained thoughts which all teachers might well think of. The oration of Mr. Perley displayed much "Moral Force," both in diction, and delivery, and that of Mr. Rollins, reminded us forcibly that "Young America" *had* honorably exerted himself, in thought and speech.

We regret to learn that the highly-esteemed Principal, Mr. Allis, and the Preceptress, Miss Brooks, an inestimable teacher, are called to another field of action. We understand that Mr. A. I. Dutton, an experienced teacher, is to take charge of the Academy, in the place of Mr. Allis. We recommend all who take an interest in institutions of the kind, to patronize Mr. Dutton, who appears a stranger in Topsfield, and a laborer in the noblest of all causes, the Improvement of the Mind.

ALBERT IRA DUTTON.

Prof. A. I. Dutton followed Principal Allis. He began with the winter term of 1858-9, and taught five consecutive terms. During his first year he had one hundred and twenty-one students, with an average per term of forty-nine. Mrs. Mary A. Jones was his preceptress and Miss Helen A. Reed, assistant. J. W. Porter and J. B. Putnam were assistants the summer term of 1859; Geo. F. Flint and Miss Lucie R. Weston the fall term of the same year. Prof. Downes, jr., gave instruction on the piano. Miss Sarah D. McMillan, a graduate of Kimball Union Academy, Meriden, N. H., and an experienced teacher, succeeded Mrs. Jones' resignation, at the end of the year 1858-9. About 1860, commercial colleges began, and local high schools, with their attractions and advantages, more or less real. Georgetown was able to appropriate more for the recognized ability of the Academy principal than the earning capacity of the Academy could offer, and he left at the end of the winter term of that year.

The program of the exhibition at Union Hall, Thursday evening, May 5, 1859, consisted of tableaux, dialogues, orations, recitations, an original colloquy and music. The Latin Salutatory (Oratis Salutoria) was pronounced by Arthur M. Merriam, and the valedictory, a poem, by M. B. V. Perley. These orations were given: Energy, Earnestness and Perseverance, by N. D. Dodge, jr.; Foresight, by John W. Perkins; The Spirit of Freedom, by B. H. Weston. The recitations: The Gambler's Wife, by Carrie E. Batchelder, and The Lay of the Madman, by J. B. Putnam. There were six dialogues. The colloquy was original and written by the Preceptress, Miss Helen A. Reed.

This exhibition was among the most attractive known in the history of the school. The hall was crowded; the presentations were most pleasing; everybody was more than gratified; and immediately following the conclusion, a motion came from the audience, that the program be repeated the following evening, which was unanimously voted.

Mr. Dutton was born in Stowe, Vt., Aug. 5, 1831, to Ira and Emeline (Dutton) Dutton, a farmer. He graduated at Middlebury College, 1858, and taught that fall in North Troy, Vt. His next field was at Topsfield, then a year at Georgetown. He studied a year or more at Hartford, Ct., and completed his divinity course at Andover, where he graduated, 1863. That year he was ordained and installed pastor of the Congregational church at Shirley, Mass. He remained there six years, till 1869. In the latter year he was installed at East Longmeadow, Mass., where he served till July, 1885. He then visited the west, for his health, and previous to Oct. 1, 1885, preached in Marshall, Minn. He began preaching in Royalton, Vt., in Oct., 1885, and in Sept., 1886, was installed pastor. In 1887, he received a carriage accident owing to which he was unable to preach, and Oct. 1, retired from the pastorate to become superintendent of the Home for Aged and Disabled Ministers, at South Framingham, Mass. He was several years a Trustee of Monson Academy.

In 1880 he sustained a severe accident by being run over by a loaded team. From this he never fully recovered. He was unable, for a long time, fully to attend to the duties of his pastorate. But for five years he remained with his parish, "accomplishing some of his best work and bringing a goodly number into the church." The last accident unfitted him for parochial duties, and he accepted a call to superintend the Minister's Home. He had been there three years when the Home was discontinued. Mr. Dutton, however, continued to reside in the place, and during the time had several calls to pastorates; but for want of health felt obliged to decline them. He was building a residence for himself and family at the time of his death. His last sickness was only of fifty-eight hours duration. He preached for his son, the Sunday before, in Ashland. He passed away very suddenly, in his sleep, of heart-failure, a result of la grippe, Feb. 13, 1892.

Mr. Dutton's wife was Miss Helen Abby Reed, his assistant in the school at Topsfield. She was born May 6, 1838, to Jacob Whittemore, a lawyer, and Ruhannah Burbank (Tenney) Reed, of Groveland. Their marriage was at Groveland, Oct. 29, 1863. Their children were born: Charles Henry, Jan. 26, 1865; Emily Helen, Sept. 29, 1869; Mary Almira, Oct. 31, 1871, and died aged one year, five months; Albert Ira, Sept. 4, 1877. Charles is a graduate of Amherst and pastor in Wilton, N. H. Emily graduated at Mt. Holyoke College, took her master's degree at Radcliffe College, Cambridge, and is instructor in Latin at Vassar College.

Mrs. Morgan thus concludes a very interesting reminiscence which we have digested through these pages:—"Very few resident students studied in school, all must attend devotional exercises in the morning, which consisted of scripture reading, prayer, and singing a hymn by a select choir of the scholars; then pupils went to their various homes for study, returning at hours designated; discipline required the incoming classes to be promptly at hand, when the bell rang at the close of each recitation.

Looking back to those days we can but exclaim 'What an excellent corps of teachers taught in the old academy!' Years have passed since we saw them, but their influence and example are still seen and felt in the lives and labors of those they instructed, now scattered throughout the world. The years have also changed the old building; its halls still echo the tread of scholars, but not after the old plan. The laugh-

Austin Hazen.

ter of merry children and youth is heard on the hill, but in them *we* see only the forms and faces of other days."

MISS SARAH DANA McMILLAN.

Miss McMillan was Prof. Dutton's preceptress, during his last term. She had graduated at Kimball Union Academy, Meriden, N. H., and had taught three years in the Academy at Plattsburgh, N. Y., and then in the Pinkerton Academy, Derry, N. H. She came to this school, a lady of valuable experience, of cultured talents, and apt ability to impart instruction. Her social life and pleasing manners endeared her to pupils and people, and after Mr. Dutton left, she remained, at the urgent request of friends, and taught, on her own account, during the following summer.

She was the daughter of Hon. Andrew and Emily (Dana) McMillan, born May 12, 1836, at Danville, Vt. Her mother was a lineal descendant of Gen. Israel Putnam. In July, 1865, she married Rev. E. G. Parsons, pastor of the First, now Central, Congregational Church, of Derry. Mr. Parsons was ten years principal of Dummer Academy, having his election in 1882. They now reside in Derry. Mrs. Parsons writes:—"My memories are most pleasant of the genial, hospitable people, who then were active in church and society, and extended their kind ministrations to 'the stranger within the gate'."

CHAPTER VI.

THE ACADEMY EDIFICE.

ITS LATENT LIFE AND MEED OF PRAISE.

Thus far we have followed the use of the building, have noted the principal teachers in their order, and most of the assistant principals, have recorded enough of their lives to show their enterprise, their moral force, their natural ability and education, their citizenship and Christian worth,—and it remains to speak of the structure itself.

The property was insured the years 1828, 1829, 1830, for $1500. The years 1831 and 1832 for $1000. Jacob Towne, jr., was treasurer, except in 1832, when R. A. Merriam served. The insurance was payable, in case of loss, to Solomon Wildes, of Boston, mortgagee. In 1833, the insurance permitted the use of the building on Sundays for religious meetings.

Solomon Wildes and his wife, Ruth B., of Boston, transferred all their right, title and interest in the property, June 10, 1846, for the amount of the first insurance, $1500, to Samuel Rea, of Portsmouth. These men were landlords. The former was located on Elm street, and the place was long known as "Wildes' Hotel." Mr. Wildes' interest included eighty-eight undivided hundredth parts; the remaining twelve undivided hundredth parts, belonging to Susan Cummings, of Topsfield, and Frederick Perley of Danvers, were not conveyed.

Samuel Rea and his wife Sarah A. C., of Portsmouth, sold their interest in the property for $800, by deed dated Oct. 15, 1846, to the persons named in the following schedule: A. S. Peabody, ten shares; Robert S. Perkins, four; J. P. Towne, two; Mary Towne, three; Abigail Perkins, two; Thomas L. Lane, two; Hannah Perkins, one; Isaac N.

(70)

Averill, one. There were twenty-five shares valued at $25 each, and included the same Rea purchased of Wildes.

To these proprietors Susan Cummings quit-claimed her interest in the property Nov. 16, 1846, for $1. Frederick Perley sold his interest to the same parties Dec. 15, 1846, for $56. J. W. Healy purchased the property of the proprietors July 22, 1854, for $800. The signatures on the deed to Healy are: Augustine S. Peabody, Robert S. Perkins, Mary J. Perkins, Isaac N. Averill, Israel Rea, John G. Hood, Thomas L. Lane, J. P. Towne, R. C. Towne, Mary Towne, 2d, Hannah Perkins and Helena Peabody. J. W. Healy and his wife Jane C., of Gardner, conveyed their interests Nov. 23, 1858, for $1000, to Albert Ira Dutton, who was then principal of the school.

From A. I. Dutton the title passed to Asahel Huntington, clerk of courts, of Salem, and Jacob W. Reed, attorney-at-law, of Groveland, and April 17, 1865, they relinquished their claims—Huntington for $1 and Reed for $1050, to Jeremiah Balch and Ephraim P. Peabody. Peabody sold to Balch, Jan. 17, 1868, for $600, and Balch conveyed the property to the town of Topsfield, March 6, 1868, for $1450. For some time between 1865 and 8 the building was used as a dwelling.

The town immediately converted the building into a schoolhouse. The number of scholars had increased beyond the capacity of the modest structure on the common, and the "Topsfield Academy" became the "Centre school-house of Topsfield."

The mission of this property, dedicated so solemnly on May 7, 1828, by the earnest devotion of the whole community, in the joyous anticipation of long life and eternal good; the mission of able and devoted teachers in helping supply the world with cultured intellects and correct and stable principles could not die. Callimachus of ancient time, wrote:—

"The good never die."

For several years the town had felt the imperative need of ampler and better accommodations for her scholars. The old worn floors and doors, the palsied windows and wood stoves, afforded no security for health and gave no promise for comfort to the scholars, and the furniture and appointments were inadequate to the needs. In the summer of 1889, all was changed; the old institution as a member of America's unique and grand common school system, took a new lease of life. The front of the building was changed from the south to the west; the old ante-rooms and stairways were removed; and the entire building as it formerly stood made into four school-rooms, ample for forty or fifty students each. Each room has a cherry-wood floor, has for teacher and scholars desks of beautiful Michigan wood, has large, fine wall-slates, and has an even hot water heat radiating from the window sides of the rooms. The front, now upon the west, is a portico, 39 feet wide and projecting from the main building 14 feet. Beneath it is the heater; within it are four ante-rooms and the broad stairways. It is entered from the south, the north, and in front. The ventilation of the rooms is complete. Too much cannot be said in praise of this amended structure. No town of equal wealth in the county can boast or be proud of a better one. It may have cost much, but it is the equivalent of the cost, and will continue modern and adequate in all respects, a joy and comfort to the student, a conservator of health and learning, and the just pride of every patriotic citizen, for fifteen or twenty years, without additional cost. The building committee were: S. D. Hood, J. B. Poor, B. P. Edwards, D. Bradstreet and B. P. Pike.

The individuality of the Academy dissolved, in 1860, at the age of thirty-two years. She had survived her sisters, except the female Academies at Ipswich and Andover—not a survival of the fittest that we know of, but she was among the last survivors of a peerage, whose demise any community may rightly, truly mourn.

That she had several attacks of "innocuous desuetude" is no derogation from her fair fame or noble worth. As well question the grace and force of Christianity, because there were the Dark Ages; or great Homer's place among poets, because

> "* * * Homer's self sometimes, they say,
> Took to his night-cap on the way."

This institution is to be judged by what she *was* and what she *did*.

Her principal teachers were nineteen in number—seventeen gentlemen and two ladies. Of the men, seven graduated at Dartmouth, three at Middlebury, one at Bowdoin, one at Harvard, one at University of Vermont while four were not college graduates. Of the latter, one at the age of ten years was reading Greek in Dummer Academy, and in due time received from Bowdoin, unasked, the master's degree in recognition of his classical attainments and proficiency as a professional teacher; another has given a long life of service to school and church; a third with his learned consort served twenty-nine years in the school-room and after her decease rounded out for himself a period of forty-five years of school work; the other bravely fought disease and labored in school and church till forty-two years of age.

Marble and Kent died at the ages of thirty-three and thirty-six years respectively, just entering upon their sphere of robust, aggressive, brilliant manhood. Of the remaining fourteen, eleven sealed the books of life at the average age of seventy-one, and three at the average age of seventy-two years are living. Long since one of the ladies passed over to the great majority, and one remains. Of the assistant principals and preceptresses we have sketched only seven—men and women bred at college and seminary.

Mark this cluster of stars that shed its salutary influence upon this Academy like the sweet influence of the Pleiades, every Pleiad like the facet of some rare gem, attractive by its own color, and brilliancy and beauty. Not that Gods eternity of space does not abound in clustered sweetness and activity: we are speaking of our own—men and women of cultivated talents, of aspiring genius, of exalted character, of great industry and lofty purpose. The achievements of their lives, their extended fame, and titled names prove our characterizations true and just. Here they gave the strength of their young maturity, here budded the promise of their sterling manhood, a noble ambition inspired their toil, fidelity crowned it with success and, though their terms of service were comparatively short, their names are remembered by citizen and pupil alike with praise. Their individuality left

its impress upon the community like the image and super-
scription of a coin, or as the signet of a king.

The course of study—now antiquated—was arranged, as
we have said, for moral culture, mental discipline and practical life.   Therein, is all of it.   The mental and moral faculties should be educated together.   Eliminate them if you
please, but to the extent of the elimination, the growth is
unnatural.   It is easier to err in matters moral than mental;
the error in most instances is more elusive, and the result is
a thousand times more fatal.   In the Academy's classical
course, the Greek Testament had a place of influence, and
the English course had its Watts on the Mind, its Christian
Evidences and Moral Science.   Mr. Vose called his school
together Sunday mornings for religious instruction.   Moral
culture was a part of the learning of those days; our times
are certainly not imitators, nor on that account more excellent.

The mental discipline of the Academy was fundamental;
it taught the scholar to think consecutively, patiently, criti-
cally; it taught him research—to follow sequences and de-
duce conclusions; it taught him self-reliance in matters of
judgment and descretion—a desideratum in the citizenship
of a republic—and fitted him—yes, to follow, but more
especially—to lead, and also taught that patient labor is the
best of life and garners best results.   The idea of the plan
was, that the fewest studies adequate to the end were best
suited to the inexperienced mind of youth; and it is a serious
question with us, if the professions, scholarship and current
life would not be better served by the old *regime* than by the
brimming curriculum of the present time.

Old academic life had its social, moral and literary atmosphere, the principal his magnetism, the scholar his ideality.
These influences were peculiar to the old academies and colleges, and may be emphasized here, since we know so well
the impressive character of the preceptors, and have thereto
the testimony of their pupils.   Indeed we are here today in
abeyance of their regal behest.   These influences are very,
very seldom, if ever, found in the public schools; they are,
however, among the most important in producing excellence
in scholarship and character.   A learned divine and academy

trustee, in speaking of the personal character of the Academy principal, said :—"This influence in many cases was even more than scholarship, as it had more to do in the building up of strong, harmonious, and well developed manhood." How valuable then, is the combined influence of magnetism, ideality and atmosphere!

Nearly 800 names of students of this Academy are recorded. Ten principals issued no catalogue. The number of ladies and gentlemen who studied here is safely estimated at 1200. A large proportion of them taught while students, and thus the individuality of the Academy began to expand. Some continued the teacher's profession, some became intelligent and progressive farmers, some entered business, inspiring enterprise and correcting methods, others became skillful mechanics, and many studied in higher schools and entered the professions. The old institution is living today in the deeds of her children; the leaven of her polemy is working through a thousand agencies, building, molding, guiding, sustaining. In biological language, she is in happy correspondence with her environment, and her life and work are everlasting as her environment.

Cried an ancient philosopher:—"Give me where to stand and with my lever I will move the world." A problem in Prof. Greenleaf's National Arithmetic, by way of illustrating a principle, calculated the billions upon billions of miles from a given fulcrum he must stand, and the next problem calculated the billions of years he must live, to move the earth one inch.

Cried an ancient philosopher:—"Give me where to stand and I will move the world," and Topsfield Academy, by her life that was and her life that is, exclaims: "Stand where thou art, and thou shalt indeed move the world, by thy diligence and perseverance, by thy integrity and ability, by thy learning and culture, by thy sobriety and character—thy manhood, by thy citizen service and business enterprise, thy philanthropy and devotion to thy God.—Hail! blessed potency, hail!

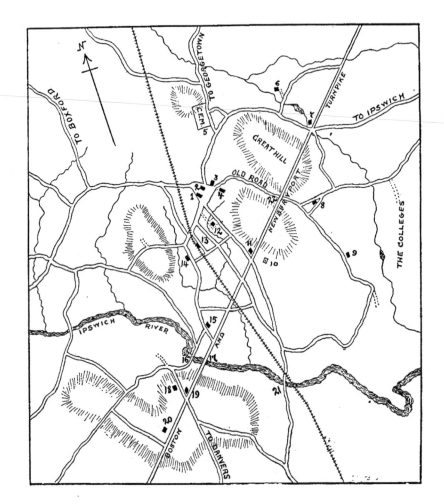

MAP OF TOPSFIELD.

1. Town Hall.
2. Congregational Church.
3. Methodist Church.
4. Parson Capen's House.
5. Pine Grove Cemetery.
6. Site of Asael Smith House.
7. Francis Peabody's Grist Mill.
8. Spot where lived Sarah Wildes, executed as a witch, 1692.
9. The Poor Farm.
10. Willow Tree. Geographical Centre of
    Essex County.

11. Site of Turnpike Hotel.
12. The Topsfield Academy.
13. Cattle Show Field.
14. Stanwood Home for Children.
15. Agricultural Farm.
16. The Wooden Bridge.
17. The Stone Bridge.
18. The Pingree Mansion House.
19. The Old Toll House.
20. The Crowninshield-Peirce Mansion House.
21. Towne's Bridge.
22. The Dry Bridge.

LITERARY EXERCISES.

REUNION

TEACHERS AND STUDENTS.

TOPSFIELD ACADEMY.

AUGUST 12, 1897.

ADDRESS OF WELCOME.

JEFFERSON K. COLE, OF PEABODY, MASS.

LADIES AND GENTLEMEN:—Before I begin my address I would like to read you a letter written by Professor George W. Atherton, President of the Pennsylvania State College.

THE PENNSYLVANIA STATE COLLEGE,
> President's Office.
> > *State College, Centre Co., Pa.*

MR. GEORGE F. DOW, *July 21, 1897.*
> Topsfield, Mass.

My dear sir:—I very much regret to be compelled to give up my engagement to meet the old Academy students next month.* At the time I wrote you last I had not the slightest idea that anything could intervene to prevent me from being with you ; but I find myself obliged to go to Europe, and shall therefore be out of the country when the Reunion is held.

---

*Professor Atherton had accepted an invitation to deliver an address at this time.

(77)

The disappointment is a very great one to me, as I had anticipated a renewal of associations which have been among the most delightful of my life.   My attendance at the Academy was the first step in my effort to secure a college education, and, while the associations then formed have been broken by long separation, it would be an inexpressible satisfaction to take again by the hand those with whom I spent so many delightful hours.   To the few who will remember me I wish you would convey my greetings, and to all my sincere regrets.

Thanking you very much for your courtesy in the matter, I am

Faithfully yours,
GEO. W. ATHERTON.

And because of Mr. Atherton's inability to be here, and the change necessary in the program, I stand before you at this time to bid you welcome.   So, classmates, schoolmates, former teachers and pupils, as I look into your faces this afternoon, changed though they are by the years that have passed, I see, I think, in each one, a reflection of that which is in my own heart, and I will say, as so many said this morning, "I am glad to be here today."   I am glad to be in Topsfield on this most interesting and auspicious occasion.

We may congratulate ourselves, my friends, on the beautiful day that Providence has given us for this gathering; and as we have come together, as we have shaken the hands of those who were our schoolmates so many years ago, and have renewed those early acquaintances, real joy has come into our hearts, and I feel that it is a gathering of which everyone present is glad to be a part.

It is my duty, as well as my privilege, to extend to you, as members of the Academy, the welcome of those whose interest and labors of love have made this coming together a reality.   In behalf of Mr. George Francis Dow, to whom perhaps we are most indebted for this pleasant occasion, I extend to you a most hearty and cordial welcome.

Associated with him are the later students of the Academy, and the Historical society of the town, and in their behalf I extend to you a most cordial welcome.

And the good old town, I do not know that we have a special or official representative of the town present, but I am sure that we have from the citizens, many of whom we remember with great pleasure, a most hearty welcome.

We are changed, but as I now look into your faces, and as I have, during the morning, met one and another of my old school fellows, after close scrutiny, and a long grasp of the hand, I have been able to say "Yes, I can see the old familiar eyes, and hear something of the younger tone of the voice," and so our hearts spring forth to one another, and we grasp the hand again and say "Yes, we were here together forty years ago;" forty and more years, some of us can say, and still we feel young today.

But the hands of time have been busy. We have changed, and the old Academy is changed. We should all be glad if we could go up yonder hill and in at the door of the Academy and see things as they were then, but the building has been changed—changed to be younger and more modern, as is fitting and to be expected, in a community like this.

But some will say, "Topsfield Academy! Why, Topsfield Academy is dead! It died years ago!" Oh no! Topsfield Academy still lives! Not only in the hearts of those before me, but it lives in our lives—in the lives of every one who hears me this afternoon. It lives in our memory of those whom we knew in those years, and who have gone on before, and whom we expect to meet sometime on the other shore.

One of the reverend gentlemen who sit behind me, said to-day that he has never seen the name of a Topsfield Academy student in the Police Gazette or a Rogues' Gallery. (He may, later on, tell you how he knows so much about the Rogues' Gallery.) But I presume he is right when he says that those who were educated in Topsfield, and took in the inspiration of these beautiful hills, and carried out the instructions given us by our kind and thoughtful teachers, have never been heard of in the Police Gazette or Rogues' Gallery.

To Topsfield Academy and its instructors we all look back to-day with pleasure and gratitude, for what we here gained in our efforts to acquire a higher education.

And, to the old Academy, the communities about here

from which we came owe a debt which, perhaps, some might say, can never be repaid, but which we may, I think, better say, has been, and is being, paid in the lives of the many who went out from the Academy so well equipped for eminent usefulness.

And the founders of the Academy,—let us not forget them, but bear in mind how richly we have entered into their labors, and how great is our obligation to them for their zeal, their unselfishness and their liberality.

And the good old town, which in so many ways and for so many years did so much to maintain the Academy! It is a source of great honor to this people that here, when public schools of a high grade were lacking, such an institution as this held so high and so large a place in their hearts. The fact is indisputable testimony to the character and worth of the good citizens of Topsfield. And the good cheer, the hearty welcome, the ample preparations which meet us on every hand here to-day are but added testimony in the same direction, and are proof to us that in all these years the character of this people has not changed, except it be for the better.

So in many ways, in many hearts, in many lives, the old times are renewed, and we who are here to-day rejoice that a kind Providence has spared us to meet once more, living witnesses to the fact that Topsfield Academy still lives.

ORATION.

BY JOHN WRIGHT PERKINS, OF SALEM, MASS.

I am forceably reminded by my position here to-day, of an incident which happened nearly forty years ago. Its story has been often repeated and is doubtless familiar to many of you. But when new the incident was this:—The late Rufus Choate had been engaged to give the Oration at the commencement exercises of Dartmouth College, his Alma Mater. Failing health had obliged him to withdraw from the engagement and Dr. Holmes had been secured to speak in his place. On the Doctor's way up to Hanover the question was asked:—"Who is to fill Mr. Choate's place on the program?" To which the Doctor at once replied:—"Nobody is going to *fill* it, *I* am going up to rattle round *in* it."

Sharing with you in the general disappointment and regret, occasioned by the necessary absence of the distinguished gentleman, who was put down as the Orator for this occasion, I have at the eleventh hour engaged to stand here and "rattle round in his place."

In the twenty minutes to which this part of the program has been wisely limited, it would not, of course, be possible, to treat any subject exhaustively, but it will be necessary to adopt a somewhat touch and go style, in the way of suggestion, rather than of completeness.

Having in mind, that we were to meet as the representatives of an educational institution, drawn together by considerations chiefly personal and local in their nature, it has seemed to me not inappropriate to take as my theme:—The Personal and the Local Element in Education. It is possible for words of most important meaning to loose something of their definiteness, by the very commonness and extent of

(81)

their use.   They seem to shade off into varied significations,
modified by the personalities of the many who use them.
Thus, Religion, Politics, Education, stand for most important principles, and yet we know that each of these words
may awaken different conceptions, in the minds of people of
the same community.   Hence, in speaking of such topics,
it is well in the beginning, to make a statement of what the
subject treated means in the mind of the speaker.   Particularly is this true of Education, since, as we shall see, the
word has two well-defined meanings.

   Some months ago, I was requested to write an article of
not more than four hundred words upon this subject:
"What constitutes a good education and how to obtain it."
I respectfully declined, giving as my excuse, that I did not
have sufficient time to cover so large a subject in so few
words.   I added, however, that for a brief and comprehensive answer to the questions proposed, I knew of nothing
better than six words from the Old Testament:—"Fear God
and keep his commandments," bearing in mind that fear,
here means profound reverance, and that the commands of
God have been written not only in a book, but all over the
face of nature, and stamped upon the individual conscience
of every rational being.   You will remember that in the
context from which these six words are taken, they are followed by the statement, "For this is the whole duty of man."
But the word duty is in italic, indicating that it is not in the
original, so that the Hebrew text is even stronger and more
suggestive, with the meaning, "For this is the whole of man."
Education in its enlarged sense has to do with the whole
man.

   Since giving that answer, I have heard a definition given by
two college professors, from widely distant colleges, and each
defined education in the words used by the other, namely,
"fullness of life," which is much the same in substance as the
one suggested above.   But this word in its strictly technical
and scientific sense is more restricted in its meaning, and de-
notes only that culture which is the product of a human mind,
working upon and directing the mind of another.   The larger.
definition given above reminds us of the words of him, whom,
whatever else we may think of him, we must regard as the

greatest and most influential of teachers in which he pro-
claimed the object of his mission in the declaration, "I am
come that they might have life and that they might have it
more abundantly." But along side of this declaration it is
well to place his other saying, "Is not the life more than meat
and the body than raiment?" and also his statement, "He that
would save his life must lose it." In these three sayings of
the founder of Christianity, we have the foundation of a large
part of the Philosophy of Education. We have its aim, an
abundant life, the suggested meaning of life as something
raised above mere material well being, and the further truth
that the largest expansion of life must come through previous suppression and self denial.

In the old Assembly's Catechism, in which our fathers were
instructed and some of us began to be instructed, the first
question and answer, you will recall, has to do with the "chief
end of man." As it is therein defined, it is not easy to see
how either part of the answer could be realized short of the
fullest development of all our powers and capabilities. For
a time, it was a question of hot discussion and patient investigation among men of science, whether in the physical world,
there was to be found convincing evidence of the spontane-
ous origin of life. But after much trial the confession came,
"We know nothing of the origin of life save as it is found in
preexistant life." So of by far the greater part of our intellectual, our moral and our spiritual life, the part which is the
product of education in its scientific sense, we have to say, it
is wholly dependant upon preexistant life of a similar kind.

Whether the man has been trained in the schools, or is a
so-called "self made man"—an impossible product, by the
way, in civilized society—in the last analysis he will be found
mainly indebted to the spoken or written word, or to the un-
spoken or unwritten personal influence of other men.

So great is the undesigned and unconscious effect of social
relationship, that it has always formed a great factor in the
advantages of our schools, particularly where, as in academy
and college, the students see much of one another outside of
the hours set for study and recitation. Edward Everett Hale,
speaking of the influences which had contributed to his education, says, for the good he received in college, he was more

indebted to the fellows, than to the faculty.   If any one thinks
that Dr. Hale does not mean to be taken quite seriously in
this assertion, it must at least be acknowledged as strong testimony, from a high authority, to the advantage obtained from
the mutual intercourse of student life.

A similar sentiment was expressed in a letter I once received from a gentleman in a distant city, concerning his son
who was under my instruction.   He said he wished his boy
to go to college, preferably to one which had a widely dis-
tributed patronage, that he might make the acquaintance of
cultivated men, representing different and distant types of
American society.

But the personal element, great as its province is, can not
claim the entire realm of education for its own, when we use
the word education, in its most comprehensive sense.   Then
the word stands for a result, which is the product of all the
influences that combined to increase one's power, elevate his
taste, or purify his character, and among these, the element
of locality, with all it implies, must take a very high rank.   In
savage life this comes to be strikingly noticeable.   Literature
and tradition are fruitful in anecdote of habits of minute observation, of mental alertness, and power of quick adaptation
to sudden emergencies, among uncivilized men, which seems
to us preternatural, not to say, supernatural.

In literary productions of the highest order, the most impressive passages are often those which reveal the power exercised upon the author by local scenery and homely incident.   Prophet and Psalmist are replete with imagery of the
open country life with which they must have lived on terms
of friendly intimacy.   When we read Homer and other ancient poets, Greek and Latin, we are constantly finding delightful evidence of strength, wisdom, and refined simplicity
of taste drawn from the same unfailing source.   Especially
can no one read Homer without being impressed with the
evidence, that he was influenced by proximity to the ocean.
One of his many descriptive epithets is so expressive and so
resonant, that from it Dr. Holmes coins a word, when he
speaks of the "poluphloesboean sea."   This, in plainer English, means the sea of many voices.   Can any one doubt, that
the man who thus habitually expresses himself, had often

walked by the shore of the sounding sea, and had taken into his soul both the awakening, and the subduing effect of the thunderous reverberation, and the lisping, tinkling melody of its music.

Among poets of our own tongue, Burns, Whittier, Longfellow, and Lowell, represent—two of them—an education independent of the schools, the other two, the highest education to be obtained by almost every appliance of culture. Yet all are alike in this, that those things in their works that charm us most, could not have been produced, had not the authors been brought face to face with Nature at first hand.

Whenever I hear—as I frequently do—children whose life is mostly confined in cities, reading or reciting gems of prose or poetry descriptive of country life or incident, there always stirs within me, a feeling of pity for their hopeless inability to appreciate the spirit of the words they utter. At such times, I think how much there is that calls for unspeakable gratitude, in the lot of one in whose early life, field and meadow, pasture and woodland, winding streams and sequestered paths, animate life both wild and domestic, were the objects of daily observation.

I still walk occasionally over the same road and pasture paths that were my daily route between this school and the home of my boyhood. They happen to lie through some of the most attractive scenery of this beautiful old town. And, as I stop here and there to gaze, seeing before me the beauty and variety of the extended landscape and the distant sea, I ask myself the question:—"Did I as a boy, *did* I, take in all these things at their full worth?" and the answer rises in my heart, that whether I did or did not, their silent influence wrought for me, that which has immeasurably increased the worth of everything else that I have ever learned. Among the blessed fruits of these country academies, we are to consider the importance of the service they rendered, in bringing young men and maidens from the cities, during a part of the plastic period of youth, into more intimate contact and acquaintance with the grand old teacher of us all, Mother Nature herself.

But the influence of locality may be felt as an educative force also, through the law of association, in bringing before

our mental vision with increased vividness, deeds and events
that deserve undying remembrance. Thus, from all parts of
our country and from beyond the sea, the thronging multitudes come to visit Plymouth Rock, and Lexington, and Concord, and Bunker Hill. They come with no expectation
surely, of being thrilled by the intrinsic beauty or grandeur
of these places; but because the places are suggestive of the
sublime faith in God, through which our country was founded, and the sturdy, heroic valor, with which its liberties were
defended.

Two hundred and fifty years ago this very year, the Puri-
tan spirit expressed itself in establishing the first free public
school in Massachusetts. The act of establishment was accompanied by a preamble which stated the motive, and ended
with these words:—"That learning may not be buried in the
grave of our fathers in the church and commonwealth."
They had already founded the college. We hold these acts
in highest honor, not alone because we regard them as the
fountain from which there has flowed, and from which we
believe there will ever continue to flow, a stream whose wa-
ters shall do much for the "healing of the nations," but because we know something of the personal sacrifice and self
denial which these acts involved, on the part of those by
whom they were conceived and executed.

But founded in much the same spirit, and often maintained
with hardly less personal sacrifice, were the country academies which dotted so many of the hills of New England, and
which did a most important work that otherwise must, in
great part, have been left undone.

Today the spell of personality, and the spell of locality,
are strong upon us. We feel that it is good for us to meet
once more, to renew our familiarity with the place, and with
one another, and to recall the memory of other schoolmates,
and former teachers, to all of whom, our feeling of indebted-
ness is deep and lasting. But the place and the occasion
remind us, also, of others, who may or may not have ever
been members of the same school, but through whose
inspiration, and self-denying help, the advantages of an extended school-life were made our own. Today, like the
gracious return of a blessed presence, the thought comes to

us, of those who judged no pains too great, no sacrifice too costly, that son or daughter, brother or sister, might share to the full in the benefits of sound learning, because they believed that in such sacrifice, they were helping to transmute the outward things of life, into the inward power of enlarged being, and because by precept and example, handed down through long lines of ancestry, they had learned and they wished us never to forget, to "look not upon the things which are seen, but upon the things which are not seen," in the firm faith and belief, that "the things which are seen are temporal, but the things which are not seen are eternal."

ODE.

EUGENE TAPPAN, ESQ., OF BOSTON, MASS.

We never can forget,
That years ago we met
   In Topsfield town.
In heart, and mind, and will,
We feel the impulse still,
Of Academic hill,
In Topsfield town.

Today we here repair,
And breathe the healthful air
   In Topsfield town.
Each field and stream we greet—
Each spot to memory sweet—
And tread the ancient street
   In Topsfield town.

Thanks for our welcome here,
Thanks for this goodly cheer
   In Topsfield town.
'Twas ever Topsfield's way,
To make the comer's stay
Happy as summer day
   In Topsfield town.

TUNE—*America.*

(88)

GEORGE CONANT.

BEAUTY.

GEORGE CONANT, OF PASADENA, CALIFORNIA.

"Beauty armed with Virtue fortifies the soul
With a commanding but a sweet control."

———

Whatever strikes the eye
  With a pleasurable thrill,
Or delights the willing ear
  And its winding channels fill,
Or wakes the soul to action
  And its finer fibres sway,
Or touches up the heart-strings
  In a sweetly brilliant way,
Has charms upon the beautiful
  In sky, on land and sea
'Mong high and low of every race—
  A key to harmony.
The harmony of color
  And the harmony of song,
The melody of Vesper bells
  To the beautiful belong.
Beauty lingers in the lily,
  Is enthroned within the rose,
Climbs to dizzy heights of splendor
  In the arch of God's rainbows,
Slumbers with the sleeping cherub
  In its cottage cradle bed,
Wakes to conscious revelation
  When fair youth and maiden wed.
Seen is beauty in the lowest
  And the highest of God's creatures,
When in symmetry enfolded
  And endowed with winning features.

(89)

Nothing can be viewed as homely
    That gives pleasure to the mind:
A wrinkled maid filled up with goodness
    An Uncle Tom both black and blind,
A whitened head packed full of wisdom,
    A benefactor bowed with years,
Unselfish children at their pastime,
    A fallen Peri shedding tears,
A mother with her firstling baby,
    An Indian girl by mirrored stream
Making her simple morning toilet,
    A model for an artist's theme—
All these are pictures full of beauty
    Pictures hung on every hand,
Multitudes greet *their* unveiling
    Admiration they command.
The world is full of things of beauty
    Everywhere within the poles,
It strikes with force all keen observers,
    It stirs them to their inner souls.
Looking from a mountain summit
    There breaks a captivating view,
Nerve-stilling thoughts course long the brain-cells—
    Nature's pictures touched anew;
The vastness of the sweep of vision
    Quickens pulse and brings delight,
And the far off landscape beauties
    Seem to swing before the sight;
Lake and orchard nestling closely,
    Vineyard, meadow, garden, rock,
Silver threads of winding rivers,
    Emerald forest, shepherd's flock,
Shadows from o'erhanging cloudland,
    Moving, fleck the valley wide,
Seas of grain-field, waving golden
    On which ghostly ships might ride.
This is cycloramic beauty
    Only seen from towering heights,
Overwhelming in its grandeur—
    Far transcending other sights,

Dimly glints the distant ocean,
　Circumscribing with its sheen
Islands on the curved horizon
　Rounding out the shimmering scene.
The vision changes: Night is drawing
　Down her curtain near and far
Sable drapery unfolding—
　Pins it with a jeweled star.
As the twilight further deepens
　Nature's symphonies resound;
Chirping insects the soprano
　Turtle doves the alto sound.
Then the silver limbs of Luna,
　One on earth and one in sky,
Vault upon the floor of heaven,
　Trip it with the stars on high.
Constellations light the ceiling
　Of the azure concave arch,
Unique figures masked and merry—
　Grand processions dance and march.
What more magnifies our pleasure,
　Glorifies the eager sight,
Than the heavenly exhibition
　Of an oriental night?
The immensity of dome
　Studded full of glittering gems,
Crowns the works of the Creator,
　Drapes his garments to the hems.
Reincarnate Michael Angelo
　In the Cistine Chapel, lives
Immortalized in splendid frescoes
　Which only God-like genius gives.
Nature's songs in quiet cadence
　Sound at night and early morn,
In the sighing pine-tree forest,
　In the rustling fields of corn.
When the frost king grasps the branches
　Covering twigs on bush and tree,
And the sun unlocks the shackles,
　How they fall with tinkling glee!

From the beauties of creation
  Lying 'neath cerulean dome,
Rising higher than the landscape
  Are the beauties of the home:
Wheels domestic running smoothly
  With no break or plaintive cry,
Love, the motive power and lubric
  As the days go sweetly by.
In the serious days of history
  When America was new,
When religion was the watchword
  And the christians were but few,
When the worshipers were fleeing
  From the tyranny of kings,
And these potentates were masters
  Of men's souls and other things,
When brave woman's deeds were stifled
  And heroines held at bay,
And men were lords and masters
  Having everything to say,
When such records were unfolding
  In the days of long ago—
Then the mothers seemed like ciphers
  But were far from being so;
For the rock where the Pilgrims landed
  Was as much fore-mothers' rock,
As it was the famed forefathers'—
  Just as sturdy, stalwart, stock.
When we think now of the hardships
  Our forefathers struggled through,
Just consider our condition
  Had not fore-mothers struggled too.
Let a painting then be issued
  Let it hang on every wall,
Representing our fore-mothers—
  'Twould excel in beauty all.
Character foremost must illumine
  Every step in life's career,
Crowning, makes the wearer fairer,
  Beauty that all men revere.

Righteous lives transcend in beauty
    Art or song or facile pen,
Reaching 'cross the silent river
    Recognized as *golden* then.
God's greatest works revolve in cycles,
    Wheeling, whirling, never wrong,
So, moral heroes have an orbit
    Which to the beautiful belong.
Men will travel land and ocean
    In search of treasures seldom found,
When all around them in the home-land
    Treasures everywhere abound:
Wonderful treasures in tree and flower,
    Mountain fastness, field and sky—
Myriad microscopic museums,
    Under our very feet they lie.
What so fair as falling water,
    Cascades leaping, foaming, white,
Mountain torrents rushing onward
    Filling soul with rare delight?
Breathing marble—sculptor's offspring
    Chiseled from his fertile brain—
Artist's soul-work, living canvas,
    Applauding we can scarce refrain.
Down in caverns of the ocean
    So profound the brain e'en reels
Find we many a field of beauty—
    A world of wealth man's skill reveals.
The beauties of Nature never are stilled
    Her cataracts thunder and roar,
Diapasons of Ocean will ever resound
    On island and continent shore.
Nightingale notes from ideal throats
    Ravish the ear and the soul,
And even the morning stars it is writ
    Took up the musical role.
Beauty glows in flowers of language,
    Pulpit, platform show its power,
Rostrum, forum, sway the masses,—
    Eloquence is beauty's dower.

Search we in Zulu or Hottentot land,
  Plunge we in African shade,
Climb we above the glacial flow,
  Spectacular shows are arrayed.
There is beauty of color, beauty of form,
  Beauty of figure and face,
Beautiful thoughts—the mosaics of mind,
  Beauty of manner and grace.

Scriptural beauties hung on biblical walls,
Charm us, inspire us and sorrow forestalls;
Prophets and saints, historians, kings,
Have given to thought most beautiful wings;
They flash on our vision as we scan the pure pages,
"The beauty of holiness" has been noted for ages,
'Tis woven in story, repeated in song,
Inspiring the feeble and righting the wrong;
"How beautiful on mountains are couriers' feet
That bring us glad tidings," and goodness replete.
"The beautiful temple," "the beautiful gate,"
The beautiful home *we* anticipate—
All thrill as with hope of a life that is newer,
Cementing our friendship and making it truer.
Now ere we dismiss this delight-giving theme
There uplifts before me a kind of day-dream;
A landscape so fair rises full on my sight,
Its loveliness rare the muses invite.
A village I see as a crown to the field,
Her emerald robes in beauty revealed,
Enfringed by a radiant meandering river
Benign benefactions exhaling forever,
Reflecting a joy like the "Vale of Cashmere,"
A bucolic scene that scarce has a peer.
Here the bees of Hymettus voice their sweet coming
As they bring in the nectar with musical humming—
The robes, the field, the bees and the stream
Roseate and sun-kissed make up the day-dream.
Oh! Topsfield! Top of the fields, and pride of the hills,
Tranquil and restful panacea for men's ills,

Greeting Aurora, as she mounts her red car,
For a drive thro' the gates of the morning afar;
Smiling with sunshine, smiling in shade,
Foremost in peace, but in war not dismayed,
Sitting as Queen in this beauteous valley,
Gracious to guests that 'round your feet rally!
Villas, meadows, and river your arena bedecking
With garden and orchard—your verdant slopes flecking,
Your firesides aglow with contentment and peace—
May your sky as today from gloom have surcease,
And more than all this may the stars on you shine
Lustrous in beauty as in days of "lang syne."
The day will soon close, but in mem'ry to exist,
Our lessons recited, the school be dismissed,
Yet the greenness of age must prove no delusion
Can we only accept these words in conclusion:
In "Union there's strength" in reunion yet more,
The latch string has beauty when it hangs out the door;
The reunion of hearts as the world ever stands
Is more beautiful still than reunion of hands.
Tho' the gathering years make the outside grow old
And the teeth leave their moorings or are yellow with gold,
Tho' the heads become silvered and the backs have a bend,
And the steps get a sort of irregular trend,
Tho' all of these sign-boards point but one way
Down the slippery life-slope to physical decay,
Yet ever triumphant the *heart* should be young,
Tho' the faculties falter soul-songs should be sung—
And here is a truth above all contradiction
(And as we look on this group it becomes a conviction,)
That the fairest of things—the most beautiful sign,
Is the eternal spring just below the snow-line.

Then reenforced be our courage
    As we go down the grade,
Let us think not of sorrow to-morrow,
    Nor look we to witness the evening star fade
Or ever a heart trouble borrow.

So, let the crown of all beauties
  That the reason must sway,
Be placed on the youthful
  Re-unionist today—
The one who *feels* youngest
  The laurel should crown,
For he's rising the slope
  As others go down.

———

HISTORICAL ADDRESS.

M. V. B. PERLEY, OF IPSWICH, MASS.

———

The Historical Address, delivered by Mr. Perley, at this point in the literary exercises has been entirely rewritten, and is printed herewith as a "History of the Academy." "The structure of the address has, in preparation of this history, been demolished, and the framework used as the receptacle of any and all obtainable facts having reference to the subject."

REMINISCENT ADDRESS.

REV. GEO. L. GLEASON, OF HAVERHILL, MASS.

Great interests are affected sometimes by trivial incidents. Great occasions are determined by seemingly insignificant events. This illustrious gathering once hinged upon the simple circumstance, that J. Warren Healy knew how to advertise. And this art he understood to perfection. Here, I desire to say in passing, that I agree with the historian of the day, in regarding J. Warren Healy as a most remarkable man. He was not a scholar, or man of literary culture. He never had time for thorough literary training. During his college course, he supported himself and wife, by teaching and preaching, and ever after he was engaged in the most intense service. Yet he was a peer of literary men, and for a time was the president of a university. For the same reason, he was not a profound theologian, still, he occupied some of the commanding pulpits of the Interior, and received the degree of D. D., from a respectable western college. No one would regard him as eminent for piety. Yet, he was called to the pastorate of Mr. Moody's church in Chicago, where spirituality was regarded as the prime factor. He occupied other important positions, and his whole career may be regarded as phenomenal. My acquaintance with Mr. Healy began in the autumn of 1853, and continued with more or less intimacy up to the time of his death. I have already remarked that Mr. Healy knew how to advertise. This was one of the secrets of his success. In the summer of '53' he announced to the youth of northern N. H., and Vt., that he had taken Bath Academy, and was prepared with an able corps of teachers, to give the best possible education, in the shortest possible time, and at the

(97)

least possible expense. This was the school we all wanted
to attend. The youth of that day were in greater haste to
get into their life work, even, than the young men and women of the present.

My older brother and myself, passed by an academy which
we had previously attended, and which we knew to be well
equipped and manned, and with sixty or eighty other youth,
in the autumn of '53, entered Bath Academy. We found it
an old dilapidated building, with no apparatus, and no provision for boarding the students. The able corps of teachers
consisted of J. Warren Healy, A. B., as principal, Mrs. J. Warren Healy, as preceptress, and a small limb of the law as assistant. Mr. Healy soon became seriously ill, and the school was
left to run itself. Here my real acquaintance with Mr. Healy
began, for I was one of the students drafted into service as a
watcher and then as a nurse. I found him to be a very irrita-
ble and uneasy patient, caused largely by the nature of his
disease. And here I discovered another life-long obstacle
with which he had to contend, physical infirmities which
would have disheartened and paralyzed the endeavor, of one
less brave and ambitious. The state of his health compelled
him to abandon the school, about the middle of the fall
term, and the most of the pupils left the academy. Here, I
first met Dan Wilkins, a typical Vermonter, though born
on the east side of the Connecticut river. He was a man
of unusual ability, his talent partaking of the nature of
genius. Had he not lacked some of the moral elements, he
would have been a great character. He followed Mr. Healy
to Topsfield in the autumn of '54' and, I think, remained
through the winter. He wrote me such glowing descrip-
tions of the town and school, that I decided to join him in
the fall of '55' He arranged to meet me at Middleton, as the
trains did not connect so that I could reach Topsfield in a
day. Vividly do I remember landing on the platform of
the lonely station in Middleton, one hot, dusty afternoon in
September, and looking in vain for my friend. If ever I experienced the sensation of homesickness, it was, when walking
the dusty turnpike to Topsfield in company with a Mr.
Lake of that town. With Goldsmith's traveller, I "dragged
with each remove a lengthening chain." The exaggerated

account of the town and people, and the school, by which I was entertained, did not reassure or comfort me. Here I should remark, that Wilkins had engaged to meet me at Middleton on a certain day, but I was detained, sent him a telegram in ample season, but it did not reach him until several days after I had been established as his room-mate, in the home of Mr. Israel Rea. The autumn of '55' passed without special incident. I devoted myself to earnest study, and sought to adjust myself to my new surroundings. But, at the beginning of the winter term, I became a member of Mr. Healy's family. It came about in this wise. On entering the academy, I sported a gold watch, chain and fob. This became the admiration of some, the envy of others, and the scorn of a third class. I did not feel quite at ease in this gorgeous array. But Mr. Healy seemed to covet the outfit, and we entered into the following written agreement, viz.: I, the party of the first part, covenanted to make over to him the watch, chain and fob; he, the party of the second part, agreed to furnish me with board a certain number of weeks, and tuition a certain number of terms. George Pierce of Marblehead, became my room-mate. He was then studying with reference to the Christian ministry. During this term some significant, and many amusing incidents occurred.

A prayer meeting was started in the academy, and Mr. Richardson the assistant teacher, invited me to attend and conduct the singing. It was at the first meeting that I decided to enter fully upon the religious life, and publicly declared my purpose. Thus was changed the whole current of my life. Others took a similar stand, and the whole school, for a time, was pervaded with a strong religious sentiment. My room-mate proposed, sometime during the winter, that we should try and correct each the others dialect and ungrammatical expressions; his speech, smacked of the sea, mine, of the mountains. This arrangement worked admirably for a time. It was a great advantage to see and hear ourselves, as another saw and heard us. But a rivalry arose, not altogether generous, I fear, as to who should detect the most faults, and soon there was a sting in the criticism, some irony, and more bitterness in our corrections and we eventually lapsed into silence. After matters had come to such a pitch, we concluded to leave each, to correct his own faults of speech and conduct, and friendship was restored. The character of the board furnished us that winter was very unsatisfactory, the supply was not equal to the demand, and the quality was as objectionable as the quantity. Mrs. Healy was always overworked. With a single servant, she was expected to provide for her large and hungry family, and still do duty as preceptress in the academy, then at its height of popularity and attendance. Some of us were accustomed to supplement our meagre fare at the table, by a nocturnal visit to the kitchen. We had already secured the good-will of Ellen, the cook, and maid-of-all work, who aided and abetted our predatory warfare on the larder.

One evening, if so late an hour as 11 P. M. may be called evening, several of us were regaling ourselves with a sumptious repast after our day's abstemiousness, when a ghost appeared upon the stairway, and the most of us were thrown into a state of consternation. But Ellen, who was always equal to the occasion, seized the ladle, and hastily filling it with cold water, discharged its full contents at the ghost as it vanished at the head of the stairs. A conspiracy of silence seemed to follow this occurrence, and it is with some hesitation, after forty-two years silence, that I give the facts to the public. Personally, I do not believe in ghosts. But I am sure in regard to this one. Like others it was arrayed in white. Like the typical ghost it remained silent. But unlike others, it came from above, went back to its own place, and never again appeared.

Sam. Fowler took his dinners at Mr. Healy's. One day Mrs. Healy had cut the two pies just so they would go round. She asked each of us in turn, which we would have, squash or apple. Our replies were governed, not by our tastes or the merits of the pies, but by the prospect of their holding out so as to go round. When Sam.'s turn came, he was equal to the occasion, and replied, "I will take a piece of both, if you please." Thus, some one had to go without, probably, Mrs. Healy.

It was during this winter, that George Pierce proposed a drive to Bradford, to spend the day. He suggested that it would improve our manners to go more into good society. The real object, however, was to visit Bradford Academy, and to see one Susan Perley, of Danvers, whom he had met, and of whom he was somewhat enamored. We secured a fine horse and sleigh, with a merry string of bells, of Frederic Merriam. But the horse proved to be a tearer. He started from the stable like a cannon ball, but unlike a cannon ball, his speed did not diminish as the distance increased. However, we reached our place of destination without incident. We called on Benjamin Greenleaf, whom we found a most genial, entertaining man; his daughters were equally engaging. I had conceived a decided prejudice against Mr. Greenleaf, because of his mathematical works, his algebra had been my special abhorrence. But ever after this I have "esteemed him very highly in love," for what he was, but not for "his works' sake." We spent the day very delightfully, and profitably, in company with the students of the academy, and towards night turned our faces homeward. But if the horse was eager to reach his place of destination in the morning, he now seemed frantic. It required all our energy to keep him under control. Soon the darkness shut down upon us. Another terror was soon added, for a blinding snow storm set in. All we could do was to hold on, sometimes with our combined force, and plunge into the gathering gloom. At one time, when the horse was at the height of his speed, and I was taking my turn at holding on, the sleigh gave a lurch to one side, and George rolled out. Summoning all my energy, I succeeded, in a seasonable time, in bringing the horse to a halt. George came up after a time, puffing and groaning, declaring that he feared his shoulder was dislocated. I asked him why he had got out? He said he feared the sleigh was going to tip over. I told him that never in the country were we accustomed to get out until we were sure of a tip-over. But he had incapacitated himself for "holding on," and I drove the remaining distance without further incident. It was to both of us a memorable day.

The assistant teachers in the Academy were men of rare ability and excellent character. I would gladly speak of each in turn, if time permitted. J. Henry Richardson was the assistant, in the years '55-6. I shall never cease to be gratified that it was my lot to fall in with such a pure and noble man, at this formative period of my life.   He took me into his confidence and friendship.   We walked, and talked, and sang together, and became intimate companions.   He invited me to go with him to Andover, where he had an engagement as leader of the Episcopal choir.   He took me to the home of Prof. Stowe, and introduced me to my subsequent theological teacher, and his then famous wife.   He also invited me to go with him to North Reading, to attend a concert given by the Normal Musical Institute, which was under the direction of Lowell Mason and George F. Root.   Webb presided at the organ, the most accomplished organist I had ever heard. He proposed to pay all the expenses, making the only condition of my acceptance, that I should invite two young ladies whom he designated, Miss Georgie Dorman and Miss Addie Rea.   We took tea at his home in Middleton, and his brother and two sisters accompanied us to the concert.   I afterwards became a pupil in this Institute, and was in the chorus that furnished the music at the Andover Theological Seminary anniversary.   We sang the Hallelujah Chorus with grand effect.

Some of my most pleasing reminiscences, are in connection with the families and homes of the citizens of Topsfield. I will confine my remarks strictly to my student days, and can mention only two families, that of Mr. Benjamin Kimball and Mr. B. P. Adams.   Sometimes, for months together, I spent an evening each week in the home of Mr. Kimball, the most of the time was passed in singing.   Mr. Kimball had one of the most beautiful bass voices to which I ever listened, and I have often thought that I never heard an alto voice, that surpassed that of Miss Hattie's, in tenderness and sweetness. Miss Deborah, sang the contralto, and I carried the tenor. Miss Susie, no less musically gifted than the others, presided at the piano.   But they have all gone, and I have no doubt there is sweeter music in heaven because of their presence, and I shall always be gratified that it was my lot, when a mere lad, to be invited to such a genial musical home.

Mr. Adams was the post master and kept the village store. He was a very companionable man, and often took me for a drive, and frequently invited me to his home.   I remember when the new piano was purchased. After a little I was invited in to hear the children play. Mary acquitted herself greatly to the satisfaction of her mother, and her performance elicited general applause. But Mr. Adams was greatly interested in the playing of Bennie, who promised, as he thought, to be a musical genius. The little fellow climbed upon the music stool, and with two fingers, played "Peter, Peter, pumpkin eater, had a wife and could'nt keep her," in a manner which greatly delighted his fond parents. I joined heartily in the applause. I have since listened to the juvenile performance of many a promising musician, and shared the admiration of doting parents, but never did I carry away such a vivid picture, as that of little Bennie.

In those early days of my connection with the academy, the lyceum was in a most flourishing condition. The citizens took a deep interest in the debates, and some of them were participants. Mr. Samuel Hood, who was a most remarkable man, both in gifts, attainments, and the ability to state his convictions, the Adamses, Peabodys, Balches and others, took part in the debates. Occasionally Mr. McLoud came in, and when he and Mr. Healy were opponents, the sparks would fly, and excitement was great. One amusing incident occurred one evening, during one of the debates. Mr. Richardson, the assistant principal, was accustomed to wear a tall hat. He had just purchased a new one, and, for its careful preservation, he placed it on one of the seats. Mr. B. P. Adams came in, and sat down plump, on the new hat. It was ruined completely, and never again appeared on the street.

In the autumn of '56' occurred the Fremont campaign. The three Balches and myself, started a campaign quartette. Their voices were very heavy, and mine was comparatively weak, and seemed like a little purling stream in the meadow, by the side of three roaring Niagaras. But I contributed a campaign song, which was some compensation for my failure to be heard. We succeeded in carrying Topsfield, and Massachusetts, and, I think, New England, but not the whole country.

Dud. Pearson and I, were accustomed to sing a good deal together. He had an excellent bass voice, of which I have many times heard during the last forty years. We made several attempts to serenade our lady friends. I remember one evening in particular. We had made special preparation; it was a beautiful night, and we expected to elicit great applause. He, could go very low and I, could manage to get up pretty high. We sang a song closing with the words, "Sleep, O! sleep!" After doing our best, we listened for some response, but she slept, and slept!

I must content myself with a few incidents in our school life. Our rhetorical exercises Wednesday afternoons were great occasions. Mr. Healy was then at his best. His criticisms were often amusing, sometimes terrific. We had some good speakers. George Pierce, N. T. Kimball, Clarence Fowler, and others, always commanded attention. Some also were conspicuous by their awkwardness and failures. One afternoon, Blaisdell, from Marblehead, declaimed a piece in which reference was made to the advancement of civilization. He had taken his position at the extreme rear of the platform, and when he came to this passage, he folded his arms and took several long and deliberate strides towards the front of the stage. When he was through, Mr. Healy pounced upon him. He said, "Blaisdell, didn't you know better than that? I would as soon think of sitting down on the stage to personate the sun's setting, as to stride across the platform to represent the progress of civilization." We had some excellent writers among the young ladies. Georgie Dorman always secured attention when she read her composition. She was a gifted girl and a most remarkable writer. Ellen Kimball, Addie Rea, and Julia Spiller, were always interesting. So also was little Lottie Perkins. We wondered how so small a girl could write so large a composition.

Many incidents in our school life come to me with great vividness. I commenced the study of Greek, in company with Arthur Merriam and Helen McLoud. Arthur always seemed to me to be more interested in Helen than in his Greek grammar. He later was a fine scholar. She seemed to get hold of the principles of a new language by instinct, and learned the characters from sight. Never did I meet one, whose classical insight I was more inclined to envy, for Greek was to me, for a long time, a dead language. We had for our instructor Austin Hazen, a very youthful but most accomplished teacher, and withal, a most gifted and beautiful man. Coburn Porter was my classmate in geometry. He was a very modest youth, and his head seemed to be too far ahead of his shoulders. I do not remember that he ever spoke to me during the weeks we were together. But he always had his lessons. I thought then, and time has not greatly modified my opinion, that he was the most remarkable mathematician I had ever met. His figures on the board were faultless, and he never hesitated or tripped in the demonstration of his propositions. But as there is an end to all things, so must there be a close to these recollections. Graduation day came at last, and four of us young men left the academy to return no more. Sidney Merriam and N. T. Kimball went to Dartmouth College, and Sam. Fowler and I went to Amherst. I presume we all made eloquent and impressive addresses, but I do not recall them now. The music for the occasion was furnished by a quartette, composed of Mr. Allis, who had a fine bass voice, Mr. Sumner Perkins, Mr. Winslow, and myself. It was a success, and elicited hearty commendation, which was to me, a great satisfaction, for I had, from my connection with the academy, been identified with its musical interests.

One incident connected with the evening entertainment was both characteristic and amusing. It seemed to be a proper thing, for the young people to pair off at such an important epoch in their lives. Choice, instinct, and natural selection, helped in determining the selection, with the most of us. But none of these sentiments influenced Sam. Fowler. He waited until all the young ladies had been provided for, and took the one who was left. After he had walked a reasonable distance, he learned that the aforesaid young lady lived three miles away. Accordingly he plodded on in silence until he had gone, what he estimated, was half the distance, when he turned back with the remark, "You will get home as soon as I will, so I will bid you good night." Sam. is now living alone in one of his tenements in Danvers, and I am not informed that he has ever started to walk home with a young lady, since the memorable night of his graduation from Topsfield Academy.

Fellow schoolmates and friends of former years. This is

one of the most memorable and delightful occasions of our lives. This faultless summer day, is an emblem of the sunshine and gladness in our hearts. The most pleasing recollections, come thronging back to our memories, and we live over again the joys of our youthful days. Faces wreathed with smiles, come out of the shadows of the past. Forms, once so dear to us, long since passed within the veil, come before us in glad review. The chain of friendship, severed by a period of forty years, is now reunited, never again to be sundered, not even by death. The lines of toil, and care, and age, and perchance of suffering, are furrowed in our faces, but still the lineaments of youth remain. But our hearts are as youthful, and beat with as cordial sympathy for each other, and loving loyalty for the old Academy, as when we parted, nearly half a century ago. Do not our hearts burn within us, as we here review, 'mid smiles and tears, the long procession of the years.

ADDRESS.

JUDGE ISRAEL W. ANDREWS, OF DANVERS, MASS.

MR. PRESIDENT, LADIES AND GENTLEMEN:—

I had rather be excused, than, at this late hour, endeavor to interest you with what I might have to say, but, for the few minutes allowed, I shall have to amputate the speech I should ordinarily make, and so perhaps you will remain until I am done.

Yes, I was a student of Topsfield Academy in 1840-41, and I remember well, and with great pleasure, many of the associations of that day.

It happened on election day, that I was allowed the privilege of waiting upon a young lady. It seems that there was a decided objection, on the part of Mr. Healy, in regard to the young men waiting upon young ladies, and that reminds me of a little incident that occurred in New Hampshire. I went there to school before I came here. It was a Baptist Theological School and Academy—of course I went to the Academy. My father was a minister, but I never had any inclination in that direction. In fact, from what I have seen sometimes, I have thought that a theological education could be well dispensed with, even by our ministers.

I was going to say, that in this incident I met a Professor gallanting around with two young ladies, and he, the next morning, gave me a very severe reprimand for being out— it was Sunday.

Well, it afterwards happened that I was waiting upon a young lady, and as soon as it was discovered, I was promptly called before the Board, and asked if I did not know the rules of the school. I replied that I knew them all very well. "Well," said the Professor, who was also the President, "it is against the rules of the school, for a young man to wait upon

(107)

a young lady." I asked him if it was any more against the rules of the school, for a young man to wait upon a young lady, than it was for a professor. The result was that I was finally suspended, but not for that reason alone, however.

But to be serious. I have a single word more to add. I would like to say to all who hear me, that, ahead of wonderful achievements, there is a depth of thought—a vastness in the direction of man's investigation of true study.

I wrote a lecture once, or tried to, and thought I did, upon, "What Constitutes Good Scholarship, or, a Student's Work, and What He Should Do." That lecture is somewhere around the house now. I have not seen it for many years, although I have a lot of books and other collections, and presume it is there, but I think, that in view of the vastness of the problems that are arising, that our school education is becoming comparatively of little importance. I say this, and I say more—I think myself, that the academical institution, is the equal, if not the superior, of our high schools. And it is not because I am in the least prejudiced. It is simply what I have thought from my experience.

Now, we have a high school in Danvers, and the people of Topsfield have become acquainted with the course pursued, as they have sent a number of their children there.

I think there was more freedom of thought, in the academical institution, and thereby securing, better scholars than we get now. At the present time they are full of frivolous matters, and sometimes those that are dangerous to their own health, and to the character of humanity.

ADDRESS.

GEORGE CONANT, OF PASADENA, CALIFORNIA.

MR. PRESIDENT :—

I did not know that I would be called upon to speak, and I don't know as I can interest the audience, unless, perhaps, I refer to a debating society we had forty-five years ago.

We had such men in the society as Rev. Anson McLoud, Charles Holmes, Sam. Todd, and B. P. Adams. On a certain occasion the question was rather interesting to me, and I, being President, and wishing to talk on the question, left the chair to Rev. Mr. Bailey. The debate went on in a certain line, and Squire Holmes, as we used to call him, being always very ready to talk, and being also very sarcastic, and sometimes a little obnoxious, put a great many restrictions on the ruling of Mr. Bailey. Well, Mr. Bailey took offence, and concluded he had better give up his position as President, and so, while Mr. Holmes was interjecting a little of his bitter talk, Mr. Bailey stepped down, and stepped out of the chair. As he went down the steps, Square Holmes flourished his hands and said, *Sic transit gloria mundi* (Thus passeth the glory of the world), which made the incident quite dramatic.

At another time in the society, Mr. B. P. Adams, a prominent merchant of Topsfield, and a strong supporter of the academy, was called upon to speak.

Now Mr. Adams was a good talker and a ready debater, but on this occasion he did not seem ready, and rose to excuse himself from speaking, with much deliberation. He said he thought he could not give a better reason, for not responding to the call to speak, than to quote the dying words of Ex-President Adams, by saying, "This is the last of the Adams's;" and had he sat down then and there, as it was remarked afterward, Mr. Adams would have made the greatest hit of his life, but, alas! the supreme opportunity passed, and the "last of the Adams's" went on with a long speech.

(109)

ADDRESS.

REV. ALFRED NOON, OF BOSTON, MASS.

It is difficult to conceive how my name was discovered upon the annals of the Academy, and it must have needed a very close scrutiny, on the part of the Secretary, to identify the name with the present speaker.

An effort was made the other day to ascertain how it came about that I was a student of the Academy. Some of you may remember the occasion of my being here, was, because I was a boy living away from home with Rev. Stephen G. Hiler, who came from the old Batchelder place, up town, to occupy, for a few months, the pulpit of the Methodist church and the Methodist parsonage.

During that time, somehow, I seemed to have been enrolled as a student in the Academy, possibly to relieve Mr. Sumner Perkins, who was then teaching the Centre school, here on the green. There are two or three reminiscences connected with these years that come to me.

There were a good many people in the town who differed from some of us. We all have our notions, but they differed from us in publicly acknowledging theirs. One Sunday, the bell of the Congregational church, of the Methodist church, and of the old Academy, all rang for religious services. It seems that in a few hours the people expected the world to come to an end. They made a mistake, however, as we all do, frequently, in these days. The occurrence was one a great many of the residents will recall.

I remember well, the lessons in geography, at the Academy, taught by Mrs. Healy, I think, and what interesting times we had, studying the well remembered wall maps. I was one of the younger students, and remember my experi-

(110)

ences in learning long division, when we would work some simple example, and make it nearly as long as ourselves.

I did not have time to look up the old catalogue of the Academy in my private library, and hunt up the list of the names of my fellow students, but here, today, I am meeting many of them, and have renewed old acquaintances and friendships. I am very glad of the opportunity of seeing, today, the students of the time-honored Topsfield Academy.

SENTIMENT.

EUGENE TAPPAN, ESQ., OF BOSTON, MASS.

Mr. Tappan offered the following sentiment, time not permitting an intended address:—

"I prize Topsfield Academy, for cultivating a love of Nature, a spirit of original investigation, and a taste for literature."

AULD LANG SYNE.

Should auld acquaintance be forgot,
　And never brought to mind;
Should auld acquaintance be forgot,
　And songs of auld lang syne.
For auld lang syne we meet to-day,
　For auld lang syne;
To sing the songs our fathers sang
　In days of auld lang syne.

We've passed through many varied scenes,
　Since youth's unclouded day;
And friends, and hopes, and happy dreams,
　Time's hand has swept away;
And voices that once joined with ours,
　In days of auld lang syne,
Are silent now, and blend no more
　In songs of auld lang syne.

Here we have met, here we may part
　To meet on earth no more;
And we may never sing again
　The cherished songs of yore;
The sacred songs our fathers sang,
　In days of auld lang syne;
We may not meet to sing again
　The songs of auld lang syne.

But when we've crossed the sea of life,
　And reach the heav'nly shore,
We'll sing the songs our fathers sing,
　Transcending those of yore;
We'll meet to sing diviner strains
　Than those of auld lang syne;
Immortal songs of praise unknown
　In days of auld lang syne.

LETTERS RECEIVED.

Among the many Letters received from former teachers and students, the following have been selected as having historical or biographical interest.

LITTLE BOAR'S HEAD, NEW HAMPSHIRE.

MR. GEO. F. DOW,   July 14, 1897.

Com. Topsfield Historical Society.

Dear Sir:—I am in receipt of your kind favor of the 10th inst., inviting me to be present at the reunion of the teachers and students of Topsfield Academy. I regret to say, it will not be practicable for me to be present on that interesting occasion. The year ending 55 years ago, which I passed as Principal of the Academy, is one full of pleasant memories. Among the students, there were many young men and young women, who went forth to occupy important and useful stations in life. Among others, Orne and Bomer; the former died young, the latter became a successful physician in Ipswich, Massachusetts, and died respected and honored in the middle of a promising career; Augustus Perkins, now in full practice in the medical profession in the city of Boston; Bartlett, for some years a successful physician, later engaged in business, now residing in Brookline, Massachusetts, in the enjoyment of a well earned *otium cum dignitate*; Gould, many years an able and accomplished teacher, and afterward a merchant in the city of Boston. There were others of whose career I know less; John Friend is remembered for his marvellous ability in

(113)

mathematics. There were Ives, and Reed, and Bradstreet, and Ruggles, all loyal and devoted students.

I regret deeply that I shall not be able to be with you at the reunion. But my heart and sympathies will be there, and I cannot doubt that the occasion will be one of great satisfaction and pleasure.

Believe me very truly yours,

EDMUND F. SLAFTER.

WATERLOO, IOWA, JULY 22, 1897.

MR. GEO. FRS. DOW,

Dear Sir:—Your note of request that I furnish some reminiscences of Topsfield Academy, for the reunion, on Aug. 12, was duly received. My introduction to Topsfield Academy was in the spring of 1830.

Principal Vose was a man of forty-five or fifty years, I judge, and Miss Ann Cofran, the Preceptress, of perhaps thirty-five or forty years. They were both very sedate, and very devout, and the religious character of the school was always prominent.

The young gentlemen occupied the lower, and the young ladies the upper room; but at morning and evening prayers, rhetorical exercises, etc., all went into the upper room, which was divided strictly by an invisible, but effective line between the two sexes. If there was any whispering or noise in prayer time, Mr. Vose could, with great facility, open his eyes and look around the room, without interrupting the thread of his petition. But the general decorum of the school was good, and he was seldom disturbed in this way. Though he was a college graduate, and an A. M., Mr. Vose was not a very thorough scholar, especially in Latin.

In his Latin class were the late Rev. Josiah Peabody, missionary to Persia, and the Rev. W. A. Peabody, Professor of Latin in Amherst College, where he died in less than a year after his inauguration.   They frequently had occasion to ask some question about the lesson, which the teacher generally informed them he would "look up," but which the pupils seldom, if ever, heard of again.

I believe I was something of a favorite with Mr. Vose; for he used to call on me frequently to hear a class recite, and to help him in other ways.   He had one particularly fractious boy, whom he often found it difficult to manage.   The master was not a very genial man, and was, by nature, quick tempered, which made it all the more difficult for him to get on pleasantly with the aforesaid boy.   On one occasion, the lad was unusually obstinate, and I was placed in the seat behind him to watch and guard him.   He was still much more inclined to have his own way than to yield to authority; and when the Principal came to castigate him, he rose up, with a ruler in his hand, to strike back, and might have dealt the harder blow of the two, if I had not caught his hand and restrained him.

At another time, the boy was outside the house and refused to come in at the bidding of the master; when we were required to bring him in by main strength.   The boy started at the top of his speed, and we after him, and were obliged to take him by his arms and legs, and force him into the hall of learning.   It did not take me fifty years to decide, that this sort of pedagogy had entirely too much of the corporeal in it, and that it was about as much of a punishment to the boys who caught the rogue, as to him who was caught.   That intractable boy is now, I learn, a practising lawyer in Boston.

But in spite of these unpleasant incidents, the general drift of things at the Academy was pleasant and profitable.   The instruction was not of a high order, as compared with the present standard in academies and high schools; but it was much better than nothing, and prepared the way for higher and better things.   There were certainly some very choice spirits in Topsfield Academy, at the time of which I am writing, especially in the upper room, with whom we were allowed to have but little intercourse.   Out of school hours we were more free and familiar, and when we met to sing, and to prepare for exhibition, at the close of the term, we were quite social.   The program, on one of these occasions, was a very choice one, and I distinctly remember some of the themes, and who wrote upon them. My own was the very poetical one of "Self-knowledge," founded on Pope's familiar line, "Man, know thyself, all wisdom centres here," and was treated in the pompous style of the famous "Essay on Man." One of the young ladies had for a motto, the pensive but beautiful lines of Goldsmith:—

"Vain, very vain, my weary search to find
The bliss which centers only in the mind."

Some of our rides and rambles on Saturday afternoons, over the hills and through the valleys, were charming, and retain their delectable fragrance as fresh as ever. Several of those who shared them have gone to join the majority,— *penetrare ad plures*, even in Plutarch's time,—but some remain, whom it would be a pleasure to greet, if such a pleasure were permitted. I may be permitted to name especially, among the living, the venerable and honored Prof. E. D. Sanborn, of Dartmouth College, Rev. George Hood, and Rev. Benjamin How, Mr. and Mrs. Ezra Towne, of Topsfield, Mrs. Clara W. Rose, and Mrs. Eliza F. Stone, of Salem, Mrs. Catharine W. Cook, of Andover, Mrs. Susan N. Tenney, of Georgetown, and others. One of the "others," Mrs. H. N. Black, of Danvers, I had the singular pleasure of meeting, two years ago, at the house of her sister, in the city where I reside, whom I had not seen for almost fifty years. We were seated together at the head of the table, of course, as the oldest of the company, though it did not seem to us, that day, that we were very old, as indeed we are not. It was a rare treat to run over the names and history of those who were young, and full of hope, when we were also young, some of whom are now gone to the other side of the river.

"My eyes are dim with childish tears,
My heart is idly stirred,
For the same sound is in my ears,
Which in those days I heard.

Thus fares it still in our decay,
  And yet the wiser mind
Mourns less for what age takes away,
  Than what it leaves behind.

But we are pressed by heavy laws,
  And often,—glad no more,—
We wear a face of joy, because
  We have been glad of yore."

I hope and trust you will have a pleasant and profitable time at the reunion, and would remain,

Very truly yours,

M. K. CROSS.

THE CHELSEA.

222 W. Twenty-Third St., New York.

MR. GEO. FRS. DOW, AND   Aug. 3, '97.

COMMITTEE OF THE TOPSFIELD HISTORICAL SOCIETY,

Gentlemen:—Although I have not received from you a circular concerning the coming celebration of Topsfield Academy, I have seen one addressed to my brother, Julius A. Palmer, of Boston, and I take the liberty to write to you concerning my brief connection with the time honored institution which you represent.

I think it was *about* the year 1846, that I was a pupil at the Academy for a period of six weeks. It was in the spring, I am not sure of the year. I remember the names of two of my companions at the Academy, one was Cyrus Killam, who afterwards had his name changed, by Act of General Court, to Bartlett, his mother's name. He became Dr. Bartlett, was with Dr. Earle, as Assistant Superintendent of Insane Asylum, at Northampton, Mass., and afterward Superintendent, Insane Asylum, St. Peter, Minnesota. He was of Boxford. Another was Wm. Augustus Herrick, of

Boxford, afterwards, for many years, a Boston lawyer. . My family lived in Boston and Boxford.

At the time when I attended the Academy, I lived with my grandfather, Major Jacob Peabody, at Boxford, E. Parish. I usually rode to Topsfield in the morning and walked back to Boxford in the afternoon. I rode on the Haverhill and Salem Stage Coach, driven by Mr. Pinkham and Mr. Hilliard. The teacher's name I do not remember, but I liked him. He had about 40 pupils, but receiving a call to a larger field, he left us, and the Academy was abruptly closed, much to my regret.

I am, dear sirs, very truly yours,

JACOB P. PALMER.

---

53 LEONARD ST., NEW YORK.

MR. GEO. FR. DOW, COM.   Aug. 9th, 1897.

Dear Sir:—I regret that imperative engagements prevent my attendance at the reunion of the Academy scholars, on the 12th.

Your invitation brings back a flood of memories, and a longing to see, once again, those whose names are familiar, but whom I have met very seldom, if at all, in these long forty years. In infrequent visits to my native town of Boxford, I always look from the train to see the old Academy building, and wonder if its interior is still as familiar as its outward identity.

Very heartily, I send an individual greeting to each of my old schoolmates, wishing for the privilege of looking again into the faces which the years must have changed as much as they have changed mine. I wish more heartily that the paths which have been so strange; and so different; and so separated; may all enter at last, "into the everlasting kingdom of our Lord and Savior, Jesus Christ." "The wish came—it hath passed into a prayer."

Sincerely yours,

M. H. DORMAN.

MANNHEIM, GERMANY.

Aug. 2, 1897.

TOPSFIELD HISTORICAL SOCIETY :—

I have just received your kind invitation, to be present at the reunion of the Teachers and Students, on the 12th inst. I should gladly like to be with you, and grasp the hands of friends of long years ago, and review again the scenes to which I often fondly revert. It is impossible for me to be with you, but I wish you a hearty good time, and Topsfield Academy—may it long live and prosper.

Very truly yours,

MYRON R. HUTCHINSON.

———

Letters were also received from Rev. Charles M. Pierce, of Auburn, Mass.; Rev. George Hardy, of Sanquoit, N. Y.; Rev. Hiram B Putnam, of Derry, N. H.; Daniel S. Balch, of Lyons, Iowa; Samuel L. Sawyer, of Danvers, Mass.; Mrs. Sarah (McMillan) Parsons, of Derry, N., H.; Rev. A. B. Peabody, of Boxborough, Mass.; Dean Peabody, Esq., of Lynn, Mass., and many others.

A BIOGRAPHICAL SKETCH OF
DR. ROYAL A. MERRIAM.

BY JUSTIN ALLEN, M. D.

Among the subjects proper to be considered by a local historical society, that of the old-time country physician occupies a prominent place. He was an important personage in the town. Great responsibilities rested upon him. Vast interests depended upon his wise and judicious action. The health and lives of the people were committed to his hands. From the beginning of one's earthly existence to its close, the physician was looked to, to preserve life and health, to ward off disease, to relieve the sick when disease had fastened upon him, to soothe and comfort when medical art failed, and to stand by at the last and administer whatever help was in his power. Through infancy, childhood, manhood, and age, it was the part of the physician to safeguard the lives and health of the people among whom he lived.

In the eighteenth century and in the early part of the present century, the medical profession was, as has been well described, a "conscientious vocation," and less a business or trade than in later times. The physician was held in high esteem and occupied a high social position in society. He was considered a learned and enlightened member of the community and was respected as such. He had the confidence of the people among whom he labored, who trusted in his skill and gave him their support and gratitude. He mingled with the people more than any other person, was present at all seasons that make up the varied experiences of life, participated in their joys, and sympathized with them in their sorrows.

(120)

It is the purpose of this sketch to give the salient features in the life of Dr. Royal A. Merriam, who was a native of this village and who spent the most of his life in this community as a practicing physician. The data from which to prepare the paper are not as full as could be desired, especially those relating to his early history, and therefore it must necessarily be imperfect.

Dr. Merriam came of good stock, the Merriam family of Concord, Mass. Joseph Merriam was the first inhabitant of that name and evidently one of the first settlers of the town. The ancestry of the family has been traced back to William Merriam, of Kentstine, in England, who was born about 1580, and died in 1635 in his native land. William's three sons, Joseph, George, and Robert, came to New England and settled in Concord in 1636.

The Topsfield family trace their descent from Joseph Merriam, the emigrant. The lineage runs thus:—Joseph Merriam[1]; John Merriam[2], born 1641; John Merriam[3], born 1666; John Merriam[4], born 1692; John Merriam[5], born 1719-20 O.S.; John Merriam[6], born 1758; Royal A. Merriam[7], born 1786. Dr. Merriam's mother, Hannah Jones Merriam, was a descendant of Nathaniel Jones, of an old and respected family of Middlesex County.

Dr. John Merriam, the father of the subject of this sketch, studied medicine in Charlton and was licensed to practice by the Medical Association of Worcester County. He married Hannah Jones, of Charlton, "a help-meet true", as records say, Sept. 23, 1782, the marriage ceremony being performed by the Rev. Joshua Johnson, of Woodstock, Conn. He came to Topsfield and established himself in practice Dec. 1783. March 31, 1784, he bought of Daniel Hood, a house-wright by trade, the house where Mr. Hood lived, known to a past generation as the residence of the late Maj. Nathaniel Conant, where he took up his residence.

Feb. 11, 1796, Dr. Merriam purchased of Thomas Foster, a farmer of Topsfield, 12½ acres of land at the corner of Ipswich and Haverhill Streets, extending back to the Batchelder farm. On this spot he erected the house that stands there at the present time. The house was probably built soon after the purchase of the site, for he sold the Conant house, Oct. 9, 1797, to Daniel Perkins, a resident of Salem.

Dr. John Merriam was well prepared for the work of his profession, as the times then were. His medical library was large for those days. From entries made in his own handwriting in books of his library, it would appear that his studies preparatory to the study of medicine were considerable, and that he had some knowledge of Latin. There is no record of his school days, but it may be presumed that he had the advantages that other young men enjoyed. He might have received instruction from an educated man, before taking up his medical studies. From what we learn of him it is certain that he stood high as a medical practitioner, and that he had the respect of his patrons and of the community in general. He had a large practice, that extended into the adjoining towns.

As was often the case in those days, with the country physician, he gave some attention to the cultivation of the land. He acquired property and left a considerable estate, and a name that has been handed down with respect.

Dr. Merriam died of consumption, Nov. 21, 1817, at the age of 59 years.

Dr. Royal A. Merriam was born in the Conant house, Jan. 30th, 1786. There is little to be found on record of his early life. But we can easily conceive of him in his boyhood and youth as taking an active part in the affairs of the small farm, assisting in the care of the animals, preparing the ground in spring-time, for the seed, planting, cultivating the growing crops, and harvesting. Robust, strong, and athletic, he took part in the sports of the time. The bicycle, polo, and the pseudo-chase were unknown in his youth, but ball playing, coasting and skating were practiced. It is known that he was an expert skater and excelled in the more difficult manoeuvres of the sport. There is nothing definite on record in relation to his early school days. Doubtless he attended the centre school and there learned the rudiments of the branches taught in the common schools.

He might have received instruction, preparatory for college, from his father, who, as we have seen, was qualified to give it;—or from Jacob Kimball, a college graduate, who taught the centre school, and who appears to have been an intimate friend of the family;—or, he might have studied with Mr. Huntington, the minister of the place, as it was common in those days for the clergyman of the parish to prepare young men for college. He attended school in a neighboring town, probably Andover, for how long a time is unknown, where he could see the steeple of the Topsfield church in his walks upon a hill near by.

Dr. Merriam entered Dartmouth College in the freshman year of 1804-5. He graduated in 1808. Nothing further can be given of his residence at Hanover, unless we except a letter from his mother, written in 1805, in which she expressed the hope that he would "always pursue the ways of virtue and holiness, and make such improvements in his studies as" would "render him a useful member of society."

Among his teachers at Dartmouth, were the President of the college, Rev. John Wheelock, S. T. D., LL. D., an able man, possessing marked traits of character in various ways, and the learned and scholarly Roswell Shurtleff, S. T. D.

Francis Brown, President of the college from 1815 until his death in 1820, was a tutor when Merriam was a student;—distinguished for genius, character and culture, as was also Frederick Hall, M. D., LL. D., afterwards a professor of Mathematics and Natural Philosophy, and a college president.

His class numbered forty, of whom three became members of Congress; namely, Ichabod Bartlett, Isaac Fletcher, and George Grennell. Four were physicians; seven, clergymen; and of lawyers, a much larger number.

As a young man's acquaintances and associates have an educational influence upon him, it may not be inappropriate to mention some members of other classes whom he must have known more or less intimately: Richard Fletcher and Matthew Harvey, distinguished lawyers and jurists; Lemuel H. Arnold, Albion K. Parris, and Levi Woodbury, Governors of States, the latter Secretary of the Navy and of the Treasury; George Ticknor, author of the History of Spanish Literature; Amos Kendall, Postmaster-General; and Joel Parker, of N. H., and Ether Shepley, of Maine, each Chief Justice of the Supreme Court of their respective States. Judge Cummins, of Topsfield, was in college with him, graduating in 1806. It would appear that he availed himself of all the opportunities offered in his day for a medical education. The son of a physician in active practice he could not fail to profit by the association. He studied medicine at the Dartmouth Medical School, under Dr. Nathan Smith, the founder of the school, one of the most eminent medical men of his time. He saw something in a medical way of the no less distinguished Dr. Reuben D. Mussey, of both of whom I used to hear him speak. He received from his *alma mater* the degree of M. B., in 1811, and that of M. D., in 1820. He became a member of the Mass. Medical Society in 1832. In Jan., 1812, Dr. Merriam commenced the practice of medicine in Middleton. While in Middleton he made friendships that lasted during his life. He had considerable practice there, especially in typhoid fever. In 1813 he returned to Topsfield. His short stay in Middleton is easily accounted for by the fact that his father was in failing health, and had been somewhat of an invalid for some years. He continued here in the practice of his profession from 1813 to 1823.

Looking for a larger field of action he went to Marblehead, where he established himself and remained nine years. The old residents of Marblehead, who remember him, speak of him in high terms of respect.

Returning to his native town in 1832, he occupied the house where he ever afterward lived. He loved and was greatly attached to his native town. When living in other places he always looked to Topsfield as his home; and although he was pleasantly situated in Marblehead, he did not feel at home there, and when he became settled in Topsfield, he was most happy in the change. He was favorably received by the people and entered upon a good practice

This narrative of Dr. Merriam would not be complete without allusion to his sister, Almira Merriam. She made their home pleasant and attractive and contributed to his comfort and enjoyment while she lived. A close friendship existed between the brother and sister. She was a woman who was held in the highest esteem for her virtues and estimable traits of character. She had a cultivated mind,—

was a fine writer and possessed no inconsiderable share of literary ability as her letters extant will testify. She died of consumption early in the year 1839.

Dr. Merriam married Adeline, daughter of Nathaniel Marsh, of Newbuyport, at N., March 12th, 1839. Mrs. Merriam was a most estimable woman, possessing all the traits of character that go to adorn a life of usefulness and high endeavor. Of their two sons, Sidney A. (Dart., 1861) died in 1876, unmarried. Arthur M. is a resident of Manchester, Mass. A grandson, Arthur, continues the name in the ninth generation.

Dr. Merriam came upon the stage of action when the medical delusions and superstitions of the dark ages were giving place to scientific teaching. Bishop Berkeley's tar water, Perkins' tractors, the jaw bone of a dog for hydrophobia, were exploded as specific remedies. Theory was losing its hold upon medical thought. Observation was coming to the front as the proper means preliminary to a rational treatment of disease. The Doctor had had the best teaching of the day. His library was well supplied with standard works, such as the writings of Sir Astley Cooper, Laennec, Abernethy, Brodie, Bichat, Louis, and volumes of a later date as they were published. The New England Magazine of Medicine and Surgery, from 1812 to 1828, in bound volumes, was a part of his library that has been preserved. These works have important passages marked, showing that they were carefully read and studied.

As far as authentic evidence goes, we may conclude that he was well equipped for the practice of his profession as it existed in the first half of the present century.

He practiced extensively in Topsfield and in neighboring towns. In his relations with the sick he brought a scrupulous regard for his professional duties and responsibilities. In the care and treatment of his patients he carefully investigated the disease, and formed his opinions deliberately and with confidence in his conclusions. That confidence was reciprocated by those who entrusted their bodily interests to his care;—a general good understanding between physician and patient was the result.

Surgery was his specialty. He attended the cases of

surgery that usually occur in general practice and performed
the more important operations, as the amputation of limbs
and operations for cataract. He proceeded in an operation
with self-possession, calmly, without apparent excitement or
emotion. Some lookers-on unused to sights in surgery
might have thought him harsh, but without sufficient reason
therefor.

His deportment in the sick room was dignified, calm, and
cheerful. He was kind and sympathetic;—his demeanor
and courtly bearing such as to command respect, and inspire confidence in his ministrations. His cheerful manner
and encouraging words raised the spirits of the sick, and
hope took the place of despondency, which is often more
conducive than drugs to the well-being of the patient. The
saying of the wise man might have been applied to him :—
"a merry heart doeth good like a medicine." The encouragement that he gave his patients and the inspiration of
hope, were important aids to carry them through a severe
and protracted sickness. He recognized the fact that hope
acted as a stimulus in restoring the sufferer to health. He
believed in the modern doctrine of the *"vis medicatrix na-
turae,"*—the agency of the vital powers to throw off disease
and restore the system to its normal healthful condition.
In this he was in advance of the medical opinion of his time.

He was interested in his patients and felt the responsibility of his position as a medical attendant;—and possessed, in a high degree, the esteem and confidence of the
families among whom he practiced. His patrons, of whom
some remain, have been wont to speak of him in terms of
respect, and expressive of their appreciation of his medical skill.

He made no lavish use of drugs. The liberal use of
active remedies, that was considered legitimate and indis-
pensable in his early life, was not followed by him, at least in
his later years. And although he did not discountenance a
proper measure of medication as occasion required, he could
carry in his vest pocket all the remedies he deemed sufficient, ordinarily, to prescribe. He remarked to me that he
could meet the ordinary requirements of practice, with four
articles, namely :—Calomel, Antimony, Opium, and Iron or
Peruvian Bark. In the treatment of disease and in the care

of the sick he exercised sound common sense, which is often
of more practical use than drugs.

An incident of his professional career was the having
medical students,—who read his books, accompanied him in
his rounds, and listened to his observations upon disease,—
thereby acquiring knowledge and training to enter upon the
work of their profession.

Dr. Merriam's attention was not confined to medicine ex-
clusively. He was interested in public affairs, and active as
a public man, holding offices of trust in the town, and as a
member of associations, industrial, philanthropic, and social.
He was often called to serve the town, probably no citizen
more often, in various trusts. He held the offices of Select-
man, Overseer of the Poor, School Teacher, School Committee, and Superintendent of Schools, and was selected to
serve on committees in the more important crises of town
affairs.

He was elected twenty-two years a member of the school
committee, and probably always its chairman, excepting
when he served as superintendent. He must have devoted
considerable time and thought to the duties of the office.

All accounts give evidence of his interest in education,
common school, and academic. When the Topsfield Academy was founded he was a resident of Marblehead. But
he came up from Marblehead and was present at the house
of Jacob Towne, Esq., the evening of the day when the
trustees met to elect a principal of the Institution, and chose
Mr. Vose. And after he returned to reside in the town, a
few years later, he had the Academy much upon his mind.
He entertained the teacher, and sometimes had him as an
inmate of his family.

From the annual reports of the school committee, when
he was a member, doubtless all drawn up by Dr. Merriam,
we learn the history of the schools; his views on their
proper management, on discipline, absenteeism, truancy,
deportment, the duties of parents in relation to the schools,
as well as his style of writing. Some extracts from the reports will best illustrate his views upon these subjects. It
will be seen that he was not backward to criticize, to observe
and name faults that appeared, and to refer to the failings of

scholars and teachers, as well as to commend their good points.

Extracts from school report of 1838-9:—

"The committee have endeavored to follow the statute as nearly as circumstances would allow, by visiting and exercising such supervision as the law enjoins. In these visits the majority of the committee have been present at the commencement and close of each school, and once or more, about the middle of such terms, as were between three and four months in length, making their visits about once a month. The Summer Schools, taught by females, gave very general satisfaction to Parents and Committee, at least no complaints of dissatisfaction have come to the knowledge of the Committee. The smaller class of pupils, taught by them, gave very honorable evidence of having had the industry and best efforts of their teachers. Improvement was clearly evident in each, and although there may have been some shades of difference, yet the Committee will forbear to mark any distinction."

Winter Schools.—The Centre School "was not so fully attended as in years previous, there being a private Female School kept in the vicinity, but it was this year sufficiently large for one Teacher profitably to attend to. This School was noted for the promptness and accuracy with which they answered questions in Arithmetic and Geography. The larger scholars did credit to themselves and Teacher. The Committee noticed with great pleasure the good order and discipline, which has in some years previous, been a subject of complaint. There was no marring or injury done to the buildings, not even a pane of glass broken for the winter. The common courtesies and civilities of life were observed to have received attention in this school, which was very agreeable to the committee, and they think if they were more generally taught in schools, it would not be time mis-spent. The improvement in reading and writing was not so conspicuous, although some very honorable exceptions should be made in both of these branches, and as a whole, the committee had reason to be satisfied with the school."

The North School "was better sustained, as regards numbers, than in former years. Answers were promptly and readily given in the several branches of study, and there appeared an unusual degree of intelligence and understanding, in the larger scholars of this school. Some specimens of composition and elocution were given, which were certainly not discreditable for first efforts. Arithmetic was the branch in which the older boys excelled, and Geography and Grammar, the girls. The most noticeable defect in this school was of voice and distinct enunciation. The order was good."

"The East School commenced with very flattering prospects. At the first examination the school was unusually full, 35 in number, comprising a large number of large scholars, who seemed ardent in the pursuit of knowledge, but, probably owing to the inexperience of the Teacher, having never taught before, there was a failure in a perfect control over the school. Some left for other schools, and other large scholars left because they did not feel able to spend more time, and at the last examination the school was very small, 13 only being present. The committee were satisfied with the proficiency of those that were present."

"The South School commenced with good promise, and was well sustained. The committee had no hesitation in pronouncing their full and unqualified satisfaction of the progress of the scholars, in all the various branches which had been attended to, and gave ample evidence of the industry and faithfulness of the Teacher. The school excelled in writing, and as a whole, was not surpassed by any other school in town."

"The schools, as a whole, have, in the opinion of the committee, made improvement on former years. More interest is taken, both by parents and scholars. The attendance has been better than in years past. The scholars are not so backward in attending on examination days. The committee have used their best efforts to manage such attendance, by treating them with more familiarity, and in a friendly manner, and are very happy to be able to say, that their efforts have been successful."

From Report of 1842-3 :—

"Sept. 20.—Visited Centre School—40 scholars. The school had advanced somewhat on former visitations, but was not what it ought to have been. There was too much evidence that good order had not been maintained. There was a want of books, partly from neglect, not having them at school, and partly from deficiency. The reading was bad, spelling not good; writing bad from carelessness and a want of fitness of the copies given them by the teacher; arithmetic not good; geography and history pretty good. One of the largest girls in school was idle and disobedient, not heeding the orders of the teacher. The teacher appeared to have given her best efforts to the work of teaching, but her disposition was too amiable and indulgent, to enforce order and obedience."

North School, Winter Term:—

"This school was found in a healthy condition, the attention and order were good, the interest between the teachers and scholars reciprocal. There was no appearance of special lessons given and conned for the occasion, but the scholars were questioned promiscuously, by the teacher, in the ground they had passed over during the term. Two of the largest boys were an honor to the school, did themselves, the school and teacher, great credit, and if they continue to 'go ahead' as they requested in the examination, they will make ornaments in society."

East School, Winter Term:—

The teacher "had given very general satisfaction; the order and attention was very good. The school had not that lively and energetic aspect that is desirable, did not enunciate distinctly; there was a want of boldness in speaking; many answers, though probably correct, were not distinctly heard by the committee. The teacher, though a very estimable man, is not quite so ready in communication with his scholars as is desirable for an apt and successful teacher."

South School, Summer Term:—

"Sept. 23.—Visited South School for the last time. 38 scholars. From the previous visits which we had made to this school, we anticipated a good deal of pleasure, and we were not disappointed. On entering the room, at this visit, the air of the whole school breathed forth the evidence of obedience, industry and reciprocal love between the teacher and scholars. A larger number were present than we had seen before, which was of itself evidence that they were not afraid of the committee, but were willing to exhibit the results of their labors. There was a better understanding of studies which they had passed over than we are accustomed to see in such young children. They had not been allowed to pass over a lesson till they had mastered it, sometimes they had spent a week on the same lesson. It is difficult to particularize where all the branches are learnt so well. It is not usual to see writing books kept so free from blots and marks, and so much effort to follow the copy, as was exhibited by their manuscripts. In such a school, where all was so well, it is unpleasant to mark any defects, and we only say that they would have appeared better still, if they had raised their voices; we could not distinctly hear all the answers to questions."

"The committee have been instrumental, during the past year, of introducing into the Centre, North and East Districts, the School Library, published under the sanction of the Board of Education. These books have furnished a very profitable source of instruction and entertainment, to both parents and children. Although these libraries were furnished by private subscription, yet they are open to the whole district, and have given very general satisfaction, and we cannot but hope that the South district, which is the only one unprovided, will yet be induced to follow the example, by furnishing themselves with this library, or some other. Books adapted to the understanding of the young furnish profitable subjects for conversation and reflection, afford pure and chaste language for the expression of their thoughts, and would serve to elevate. their minds above the disorganizing and petty strifes of seeing who should rule in school, the master or scholars. The mind of man and child is so constituted, is of such a nature, that it is constantly drinking in and appropriating to its use, either for good or evil, whatever comes within its reach. Surround it with good principles, nourish it with wholesome, with moral and scientific food, and it will exhibit the products of such nourishment. But feed it with low and debasing thoughts, schemes and plans, and the legitimate fruit of such food will certainly show itself in the conduct and character of the future life."

Report of 1852-3 :—

"We have seen a disposition among some of the scholars, to pursue those branches of science, which are far beyond their capacity, and not the most profitable for future use in their business lives. Ornamental branches are sometimes pursued before the more substantial and useful are thoroughly understood. Without a thorough knowledge of a subject we cannot practice upon and use it with safety, either to ourselves or those with whom we have intercourse. The foundation of a building should be deeply and securely laid before we attempt to raise thereon a superstructure, and especially before we undertake the ornamental parts of the structure. We should learn to read, write and cipher, before we undertake to declaim, paint or make astronomical calculations.

Reading is of the first importance; indeed, we have but very few good readers among us; readers who do not beg to be excused when called upon to read before strangers. Reading and spelling should be attended to every day, from the time the scholar enters school, till he leaves, until he can bring his manner and modulation of voice to be so much like extemporaneous speaking, or talking, that a person in the next room, or out of sight, would not know but that he was talking.

Servile imitation of others, however excellent, should be carefully avoided, by the young learner. The copy will never be so good as the original; it will usually appear constrained and unnatural, and of course be discovered.

Reading or speaking, pruned of all eccentricities by the observance of such general rules as will be found in most of the school books, should be after one's own manner; he should personate himself instead of any other person, however celebrated. When reading is brought to this perfection it will be listened to, and being better understood, will make a deeper impression. Why do we remember everything that is related to us, and forget so much that is read to us, if it be not owing to the natural manner of the relator, and the constrained manner of the reader, which diverts our attention, or at least fails to fix it?"

"The subject of irregular attendance has been so often presented to your notice, that you may think it a matter of supererogation to bring the subject up again at this time;

but we think it of such magnitude that we venture to bring it before you once more. It appears by the returns, that of those scholars whose names are on the register, but about three-fifths, or two-thirds, is the average attendance. There are some other children in the town who do not attend at all, and whose names are not registered at all, so that not far from one-half the whole school privilege is lost entirely. If we estimate the value of school-privilege at one dollar, or one-half, or even one-quarter, per day, for a child, the whole loss in the Commonwealth would amount to an immense sum. And who of us would part, if we could, with what we could learn in one day's diligent study? Although we should, any of us, be unwilling to part with any portion of our knowledge, yet I believe those who are ignorant actually set a higher value upon learning, than those who are learned. We heard one gentleman, in his after life, and who had been limited in the opportunities for learning, in his younger life, and who had acquired a sufficiency of this world's goods, make the remark that he should be very glad to refund one thousand dollars for one dollar, which should have been laid out upon his education in his youth. This puts the question in a very strong light, but no more so than is just and proper; learning is invaluable, it cannot be measured by dollars and cents."

Report of 1853-4:—

"Scholars learn a great deal from one another, perhaps in the whole as much as from the teacher; we mean in the less difficult portions of their studies. The more familiar intercourse which scholars hold with one another, and the consequent attrition of mind, elicits thought, and serves to bring into activity the scholar's own resources, and is therefore of more real and permanent benefit. One idea which a scholar gets from his own resources, or works out, with his intercourse with another, is worth a dozen, which are imperfectly understood, that he gets from a teacher. Knowledge which is absorbed, or drawn into the mind by the inherent power within, is more valuable, than that which is forced in by the aid of foreign assistance. A pupil may obtain knowledge in this way, but then it is uphill work. To be sure, he may sometimes meet with obstacles which may require the aid of a teacher to remove; these obstacles will grow less and less as he progresses, and as he gains confidence and learns to depend more and more upon himself. The most practically useful men are those who are self-taught; because what they know there is no mistake about, and they can give us reason for it, the why and the wherefore. All new discoveries are of course from this kind of knowledge, although it may be based upon previous knowledge obtained from the schools.

It will be likewise noticed, that in several of the examinations, the school houses were dressed with evergreens. This is always pleasant to witness. When such attentions are paid to the occasions of visiting the schools, and when we see the friends of the scholars present, showing their interest too, when we see that the school house has not been abused, we feel that there is good evidence that the time of the scholars has been given to something of value, that study has been an object with them, that they have occupied themselves with things which will be profitable to them in after life. On the contrary, when we find the building abused, blinds and glass broken, fences broken down, wantonly; we cannot but have melancholy forebodings; we tremble for the future prospects, for some at least, of the members of that school. School houses ought to be held to be the most sacred places next to the church. They are our foster mothers, and are referred to by all our public speakers, with the deepest interest. Let feelings of respect and reverence for these our Alma Maters, then be inculcated by parents and teachers. Let the grounds about them be ornamented with shade trees and shrubbery, rose bushes and flowers; let each family or child plant a tree or bush, and cultivate it. Let the nakedness of the house and grounds be clothed with ornaments which shall increase the attractions of the place. If the borders of the grounds only were lined with forest trees, it would add much to the beauty of the spot, and take from it that aspect of desolation, which most of them now present. Would not the scholar, while he was engaged in such a laudable employment, be at the same time cultivating the more kindly and refined feelings of his nature? Would he be so likely even to become a ruffian, and do vio-

lence to the rules of social and refined life? Would not the
stranger and traveller, as he passed, be moved with emotions
of pleasure? Would not the scholar himself feel a little
proud, when abroad, to be interrogated, whether he belonged
to such a school? All our higher schools, academies, and
seminaries of learning, as well as all public places, have not
failed to make the ornamenting of their grounds a primary
object."

Report 1854-5 :—

"We would that you were either cold or hot; that you
would either praise or censure our reports; that you would
read and make your comments. We have no doubt but that
the teachers have interest enough to look at them, but
whether the parents do, or not, we do not know, for we hear
little said of them. We have been making reports year after
year, concerning the state and condition of the mental and
moral developments of those young immortals, for whom
you profess to have great anxiety, and which you no doubt
really have, and love too, with all the ardor, which a father's
or mother's nature is susceptible, and yet, hardly take the
pains to peruse a short account of a year's teaching, whether
it be for weal or for woe; although some improvement has
been manifested the past year, by increased attendance on
examinations. We know there is somewhat a sameness in
such reports, quite as much in the external appearance,
however, as anything within. But we have in this report, as
in all others, endeavored to tell the truth, showing neither
favor nor affection. We believe this report is not all honey-
sweetened, nor vinegar-acidulated. If we have not said so
much by way of praise in some parts of the report, it is not
because we should not have been happy to have lauded every
effort for instruction, however feeble; and we think we are
fully authorized to bestow the modicum of praise, not without
discrimination, which will be found in the following report,
which is respectfully submitted."

"In the several first visits to the schools, we endeavored
to impress upon the teacher and pupils, the vital importance
of understanding the studies which they were pursuing.
That no definition of a word should be taken, which was
not reduced down to the perfect comprehension of the pupil.

A good deal of discouragement is frequently produced by the pupil's being obliged to feel his way in the dark, through a branch of study, which would be much more readily comprehended, if only the meaning of the terms were fully explained and understood."

"We would not be understood to say, that where there is a particular bias or love of any one course, or branch of science, we would not have it encouraged and pursued. Because, we believe, that especially where there is a love of any one branch, it will be more sure to be learned, and to be learned the more perfectly, and in a manner which will be more profitable to the individual and to the community.

We are not of that number that believe that the *discipline of the mind* is the principal advantage of schools. There are a great proportion of the community who get no other education or knowledge than such as is obtained in our common schools, and discipline alone would hardly meet the wants and desires of the public. After the fundamental branches, or together with those branches, if the teacher can catch the bent and leaning of the scholar's mind, that leaning as has been said, should be followed. Water will best run in its natural channel."

Report of 1858-9:—

"The common civilities, the little amenities, of life, should be more attended to by parents and teacher. Parents should require of their children on leaving home in the morning for school some expression respectful of the fact, and the child should be required, on entering the school room, to give some token to the teacher of his entrance; for children want to know how to leave or enter a room, as well as how to act or what to say when they get in. And not so little depend upon those little things as one might suppose, for first impressions are the deepest and most lasting; it is therefore quite important we should make and leave a favorable impression upon those strangers whose acquaintance we are making. They are likewise the best passport into good society and through life, and for our own benefit at least we had better pass for a little *more* than a good deal *less* than we are worth.

The want of graceful manners not unfrequently keeps in

the background those who have talents and whose real merits are a loss to the public as well as themselves. Good manners are never lost."

Dr. Merriam loved country life and took a deep interest in the cultivation of the soil. One of the principal reasons for returning to his native town from Marblehead, was to enjoy country life and gratify his taste for agricultural pursuits. He joined the Essex Agricultural Society in 1821, and continued his connection with the society to the close of his life. Part of the time he was a trustee. His interest in the society never ceased while he lived. He took a special interest in the culture of fruit, and grew many choice varieties upon his farm. In making his professional rounds, in his gig or on horseback, he greatly enjoyed the rural scenery, the cultivated fields, the growing crops, and seeing the rewards of the thrifty husbandman in the harvest.

He favored agricultural instruction in the common schools. In the school report of Apr., 1862, he writes,—"Agriculture is truly a branch about which every one should know something; for every merchant, mechanic, or professional man, sometime in his life, is called to cultivate the farm or the garden. As this is a branch of business upon which all others depend and upon which we must all fall back, it is quite important we should know something about it."

The cause of Temperance received his early and earnest attention and support. He early became convinced of the injurious effects of alcohol as a beverage, upon the human system. It was a common saying with him that every glass of liquor a man drank, shortened his life some seconds. In public meetings, on social occasions, and in private conversation he gave his influence and ready advocacy of total abstinence from intoxicating drinks. He made very little use of it as a medicine in his practice. In his views and practice, in regard to the medicinal use of alcohol, he was in advance of his contemporaries.

One station that Dr. Merriam was called upon to occupy, remains to be mentioned—that of a magistrate. The friends of law and order were not obliged to go out of town in Judge Merriam's day to get justice administered. That object could be realized within our own precincts.

Back in the 50's, the condition of society was such as to call for the organization of a vigilance committee. The community was afflicted to an unusual degree with the evils attending the excessive use of intoxicating drink; in the language of the time, drunkenness, idleness, misspending of time, not providing for the support of the family, and disturbing the peace.

The prominent citizens of the village were largely interested in efforts to suppress the extensive dissipation, and to improve the morals of the town. It is improbable that Dr. Merriam took a partisan view of the situation, but he was deeply interested, especially in the reform of the victims of intoxicating drink, and brought his influence to bear upon the side of total abstinence, as has been before noticed.

Charges of drunkenness, and its attendant evils of idleness, not providing, disturbing the peace, vagrancy, and the like, were most frequently brought before him—but accusations of theft, obtaining money under false pretences, and breaking and entering, he was likewise called upon to consider. Of course the higher crimes that were beyond the jurisdiction of his court were sent up to the Court of Common Pleas.

It would appear that the crime of stealing, then as now, was not always looked upon as very heinous. A case where the prisoner was accused of stealing two turkeys, of the value of two dollars, the sentence imposed was a fine of one dollar, and costs of prosecution.

In another more aggravated case of stealing, the sentence was the House of Correction for three months.

For drunkenness and for being a common drunkard, not providing, *et cetera*, some cases got three months in the House of Correction, while others were let off with a much lighter sentence.

In a case where the charge was being drunk and intoxicated by the voluntary and excessive use of intoxicating liquors; that the accused was a common drunkard and on divers days and times within six months, was drunk and intoxicated; that he neglected his calling, misspent what he earned, and did not provide for his family; he was convicted and sentenced to the House of Correction for three months.

It is further recorded in the case that the "mittimus was

suspended on the respondent signing the abstinence pledge and paying a part of the costs of prosecution."

In another case where the charge was excessive drinking, idleness, misspending time, not providing, and so on, the accused promised better conduct, signed the temperance pledge and paid the costs, and was discharged and proceedings quashed.

Another case of drunkenness, idleness, disturbing the peace, etc., was *nol pros.* by the accused paying the costs and signing the pledge.

Another, for a simple drunk, *nol pros.* by paying part of the costs and signing the pledge.

A case where the accused pleaded *guilty*; penalty,—costs and pledge.

Another class of cases noted in the "Court Record," was where the accused was adjudged *not guilty* and discharged.

A case where a warrant was for an arrest for drunkenness, the constable made return that the respondent was not to be found in his precinct.

A writ for the same individual issued three months afterward, was returned with the indorsement that the respondent was *non est inventus.*

As the work of the vigilance committee was carried on in secret, and its members in a measure if not absolutely pledged to secrecy, it would seem that their proceedings occasionally leaked out in some way and came to the knowledge of the suspect, giving him a chance to escape.

The entries in Dr. Merriam's "Court Record," show that he exercised judgment, discrimination, and common sense, as well as regarded the requirements of law, in his dealings as a magistrate.

While some of his decisions are to be commended by the most stubborn advocates of the forms of law, it is apparent that he was lenient in his treatment of many delinquents, who were brought before him. If the victim of the abuse of alcohol was not treated as harshly as might have been expected, it would not be unjust in the magistrate, but creditable for him, to take into consideration the frailties of human nature, when subjected to the temptation of the intoxicating cup; the deprivation by his impoverished family of the little that he might furnish towards their support; the culpability of those who placed temptations in his path, more guilty than the culprit himself, and the blame lying upon the community for not removing the cause of his dissipation out of the way.

The inconsistence and incongruity of condemning a man for being influenced by causes beyond his control, and for yielding to temptations thrust in his pathway, could not but appeal to the magistrate's common sense and sense of justice.

It must be admitted that Dr. Merriam administered justice honestly, in accordance with law, and with due regard to the extenuating circumstances of the cause on trial.

If he was not a severe judge, the community had the satis-faction of feeling that no innocent person was called to suffer unjustly.

Dr. Merriam was too far advanced in life to take an active part in the war of the great Rebellion. But, as I remember, in a public assembly called to consider the subject of enlistments, he offered to attend gratuitously, and did so do, the families of those who were about to enlist.

He sent his son into the field to help fight the battles of his country.

For many years he was the most prominent citizen of the place. At public meetings held to discuss important questions, he was called upon to preside, as well as to preside on occasions in other towns, as County Temperance Conventions. It was the custom to turn to him to head petitions and take the lead in movements looking to the benefit of his fellow-townsmen.

Dr. Merriam made no pretensions to the role of a public speaker, but was ready to express his views and opinions in plain language. I do not know that he ever applied himself to deliver a lecture, to write an essay, or to make a set speech. But on a festive occasion, where the ladies bore a leading part, the observance of the Fourth of July, and the celebration of the completion of the vestry of the Congregational Church, Dr. Merriam left minutes of extended remarks to be made on that occasion, on "The happy influence which woman exerts on society." The tone of the speech is highly eulogistic of the sex.

A copy of the paper follows :—

"In occupying the few minutes allotted to us on this festive occasion I design to offer a few remarks on the happy
influence which woman exerts on society.

It has been our very agreeable province through life to
be much in her society. We have seen her in very many
different phases and occasions, and have seldom found her
failing to support her character for sympathy, aid, and
charity, which the world has always granted her, and which
the various emergencies have called forth. Her heart and
hand are always open to the demands and necessities of
human wants and human sufferings. Her hand is seen in
every good word and work. And her power and influence
is almost unlimited; she can and does accomplish great and
wonderful things.

We need not go beyond our own country or our own
times for examples of her energies, and the support she has
given to important enterprises.

The heroes and patriots of the revolution are sung on
every 4th of July, but did not the heroines and women of
the times bear a full share of the burdens and sufferings,
which were endured, most cheerfully and hopefully, during
those most anxious and distressing days? Did they not
part with their husbands, fathers, brothers, and friends, to
do battle in the strife for independence and liberty? and did
they not sometimes do it themselves? Who will undertake
to say how great a part they had in the matter, or whether
our Independence would have been achieved at all, without
their encouragement and patience, so important for the
emergency? and what does not every good cause owe to
woman?

What has she not done for the Temperance cause, and
what for the cause of religion in all ages and at all times?
On these subjects you, Mr. President, need no illustration.

But to bring the subject still nearer home, the ladies of
our own town have done themselves immortal honor, and
the town immortal credit by the various enterprises which
they have undertaken and accomplished in the present
passing times. Whenever and wherever we go abroad, we
hear inquiries after the 'Topsfield Ladies Reading Society.'

Other ladies wish to take pattern for forming similar societies, or remodeling old ones, and particular inquiries are
made after the reading department, the selection of books
and the mode of using them, how supported and maintained,
etc., etc., giving us evidence of the impression they have
made abroad, approving and applauding their taste and spirit.

In the present movement, having a double object in view,
viz., the observance of our National birthday and the erec-
tion of a Social Hall or Vestry for the convenience and ac-
commodation of the place, for all ordinary occasions of
meeting together, they are making yet another demonstration of their unfailing resources. We probably should not
have had a Vestry for the present, had not the Ladies given
the work a propelling impulse, by devoting a very liberal
portion of their collections to this end.

This too, without lessening their appropriations for books,
of which they have some 200 volumes, and for various char-
itable purposes. And their charities are not few, if we may
judge from the frequent inquiries made of us for objects
needing aid. Their footsteps are not always seen by the
public, when on errands of mercy, they do not sound a
trumpet before them, or publish to the world their goings
out or coming in, yet grateful hearts will sometimes reveal
their doings. Can it be otherwise than that such examples
should have a happy influence on society and the rising
generation?

Ought we not, then, to encourage the laudable under-
takings of our friends, by responding to their calls, with all
the assistance which it is in our power to render, and to
second their movements in every other operation got up for
such worthy objects?

And who grudges the small contribution levied upon his
pocket, when so many of his senses are gratified and entertained? Not the appetite alone is glutted with sweets, but
the eye, the ear, the intellect, and the whole soul are all
regaled with pleasant and happy impressions, which will not
soon, we trust, be obliterated from the record which memory
keeps, not till benevolence and virtue cease to charm, till
suffering humanity shall have no need of female sympathy,
or till time with us shall be no more.

Then give to the ladies of Topsfield their just due, Virtue, Benevolence, and Intelligence."

He was eminently social in his nature. No one more than he enjoyed, even in his later years, social gatherings, and the society of young people, for whose benefit so much of his life had been devoted. They received a cordial welcome to his home, where they met on many happy occasions.

A short poem has been preserved among his papers, that illustrates the social side of his character. It was probably written and sent by a lady admirer.

From his agreeable companionship, his robust and stately form, and engaging manners, we can easily see that he was a favorite in society.

When we consider that he did not marry until he was 52 years old, and was wont to say that he "would if he could," some allusions and expressions in the facetious production, will be readily understood and appreciated.

TO DR. MERRIAM.

What, Doct., still *solus*? no wife in the chase?
    Still afraid of that soul chilling "No"?
Poor faint-hearted soul! how I pity your case,
    More timid the older you grow.

Here are blue eyes, and black eyes, the fair and brunette.
    The grave, the coquette and the prude,
From dignified Lydia to learned Miss Bet.
    "I know it, I would if I could."

See Lucia, sweet model of feminine grace,
    How can you behold her unmoved?
A temper more sweet, or a lovelier face
    Might be worshiped, but could not be loved.

Will sighing and wishing ere bring to your arms
    A damsel more charming and good?
Not a single endeavor for so many charms?
    "Don't tease me, I would if I could."

On Lucy Ann's eye could an anchorite gaze
  Nor kindle amain at the view?
With calmness to gaze on so witching a face,
  Was reserved for one senseless as you.

The rose and the lily blend on Margaret's cheek
  Her lips how with nectar imbued!
You monster of dullness, Oh! why don't you speak?
  "Why hang ye! I would if I could."

Have Lydia's attractions no longer a charm?
  Or what can have rendered them less?
Can sweetness so touching and goodness so warm
  Excite not a wish to possess?

Your sense of her merit you have after avowed,
  I protest you deserve a rattan,
Go whine like a schoolboy, "I would if I could,"
  "In six months I will if I can."

* * * * *

Sometime before commencement in 1858, the Hon. George Grennell of Greenfield, his classmate before mentioned, wrote him asking what he thought of a class reunion on the 50th anniversary of their graduation. The proposition was favorably considered. It was arranged that Dr. Merriam go to Hanover by way of Greenfield, both going on from the latter place in company with each other. He did so. He received a cordial and hospitable reception from his classmate. The facilities for travel were not so extensive as now, so that it could not be expected that there would be a large representation of the surviving members of the class assembled. The occasion brought together only three to celebrate their semi-centennial, Dr. Merriam, Mr. Grennell and, I think, Judge Spaulding of Vermont.

The friendly and hospitable entertainment at Greenfield, the meeting of the trio on the scenes of their college life where they called up the events of their student days, and talked over the experiences of the half century, the commencement dinner where the graduates gathered for their annual festival, and where Dr. Oliver Wendell Holmes and the Hon. John P. Hale were present as invited guests and made felicitous speeches, made an occasion of much enjoyment and a delightful episode of his declining years.

The professional and friendly relations of the writer with Dr. Merriam during his last seven years, gave opportunity to learn much of him in the different relations of life; to witness the high moral tone of his discourse, his genial and hospitable nature, his interest for the well-being of the community, and the prosperity of the town.

Dr. Merriam was a regular attendant upon the Sunday services of the Congregational Church, and held to the essential doctrines there taught. He was not a member of the church organization. His religion was exhibited in his daily life, and in believing and following the plain teachings of the New Testament.

Concerning his religious views I quote from a letter written after his decease by Mr. Grennell:—"I believe he expressed a sentiment familiar to his heart, in some of the last moments of his life, that 'he could trust in Christ as the Redeemer of his soul.' His letters to me expressed sentiments in accord with the above."

The evening of his days was passed in the enjoyment of home and village life, interesting himself in the state of the country then in the throes of rebellion, exercising the rights and privileges of citizenship, attending public worship, enjoying the society of friends, having the respect of the community, friendly to all, happy in his domestic relations, possessed of a competence, he came to the period when the healing art failed to prolong life, or prevent the inroads of disease, and passed away, with angina pectoris, Nov. 13th, 1864, at the age of 78 years and 9½ months, bringing to a close a life well spent.

THE MEETING HOUSE ON THE COMMON.

Town votes relating to the first Meeting House located on "the common."

Jan. 14, 1700-1. New meeting house placed on the plain by Mr. Capens; agreed to build new meeting house 2 & forty foot wide & 4 & forty foot long.

Jan. 20, 1701-2. It was agreed upon yt ye pulpit shall be placed on ye north side of ye new Meeting house, & ye Town did agree yt ye seats shall be placed after ye manner as they be placed in Rowley meeting house, & ye five seats before ye Pulpit is to be sixteen foot long & Mr. Capens Pue is to be placed next the Pulpit stairs.

June 8, 1702. Agreed that ye new meeting house should be set upon ye hill that is to be leveled for that end which is on the plain by Mr. Capens.

July 31, 1702. The four front seats shall be Made about twelve foot long.

Oct. 5, 1703. Agreed that the new meeting house should be seated after the manner as Ipswich new meeting house, leaving no room for Puese except Mrs. Capens Pue.

Granted liberty to people of the Town to set Stables for their horses on the back side of ye new meeting house, provided they set them as near the Swamp as they can.

Nov. 5, 1703. Chose Dea. Saml. Howlet, Leiut. Thomas Baker, Leiut. Tobijah Perkins, Sargt. Daniel Redington & Corpl. Joseph Towne, a Commitee to seat the people.

Mr. Tillton should take down the pulpit.

The Town agreed to Adjorn the meeting down to the new meeting house. The Town agreed to pass acts in the new meeting house.

The Town agreed that the vacant room on both sides of

(146)

ye Pulpit should- be for Puese, & agreed that Mr. Baker should have liberty to set up a Pue behind Mrs. Capens Pue, & agreed that Mr. Bradstreet, Leiut. Perkins & Mr. Isaac Peabody have liberty to set up three Pues on the west side of the Pulpit, the town reserving all rights.

Dec. 3, 1703, The Town granted liberty for Pues to be set up each end of the Pulpit. Mr. Bakers Pue for his wife & family, behind Mrs. Capens : & Mr. Bradstreet to set with wife & Leiut. Perkins next Mrs. Bradstreets for himself & wife.

Dec. 28, 1703. Committee reported on seating people, not accepted. Instructions agreed upon ; first men from 60 years & upward to be respected for their age before money in younger men ; 2d the meeting house rate in 1702 & the County rate in 1703 to be the rule to seat the rest of the people by, & Sargt. John Gould, Corpl. Jacob Towne & Ebenezer Averell are added to the former Committee.

Dec. 8, 1704. Liberty is granted to Joseph Andrews to get the Pue finished, in the N. W. corner he paying for making said Pue, & have liberty to improve it so long as he is a constant hearer of ye word of God with us, & doth yearly pay two shillings as he hath promised, yearly towards Mr. Capens Salery, & when said Andrews doth leave Town the Pue may be disposed of by the Town.

Mar. 6, 1704-5. Liberty is granted to Abraham Howe, Jacob, Daniel & Caleb Foster to set up stables.

Nov. 21, 1705. Allowed Mr. Capen one shilling & six pence, for varnishing the pulpit.

To be Sold at Publick Vendue on thursday, the 22nd Day of Nov^{mb.} Instant, at one of the Clock after Noon, by me the Subscriber, at the house of Lu^{t.} Daniel C[l]arks, Inholder, in Topsfield, a State Note that amounts to Twenty-one pounds one shilling: to the highest Bidder, in Silver money, in order to Discharge the State tax of David Balch, Junr. that is to be Paid in hard money, as it stands in my List for the year 1780: the above Note was Given in Dec^{mb.} 1777: and is payable in March, 1782:

Dated, Topsfield Nov^{m.} 20: 1781.

Daniel Bixby, Constable.

[Bixby Papers.]

HOTEL FOR SALE.

The subscriber, wishing to retire from her present active employment, offers for sale the TOPSFIELD HOTEL, with all its appendages. The spacious and well constructed buildings, consisting of House, Stable, Sheds, Wash-house, Wood-house, Hay-scales, &c, &c., are all well built, of the best materials, and are now in excellent repair. Besides a good Well of water, there is a Lead Aqueduct, which supplies the House and Stable with water from a never-failing spring.

Topsfield Hotel is situated on an eminence that overlooks the village, and commands an extensive view of the surrounding scenery, which is uncommonly beautiful. It has for many years been a favorite summer retreat. Any person wishing to occupy such a stand, will rarely find one combining so many advantages. Seven regular Stage coaches stop at the Hotel every week day and the private travel has been constantly increasing. A good title and immediate possession will be given, and the terms of payment be made to suit the purchaser.

SUSAN CUMMINGS.

For further information apply to SOLOMON WILDES, ESQ., Boston, or to MRS. CUMMINGS, now at the Hotel.

Topsfield, May 28, 1835. *[Salem Gazette.]*

Lightning Source UK Ltd.
Milton Keynes UK
UKHW020028301118
333214UK00014B/1701/P